Mackenzie King

Mackenzie King
Man of Mission

by William Teatero

A Personal Library
Publication, produced
exclusively for

Nelson

Mackenzie King

Personal Library
Publishers
Suite 539
17 Queen Street East
Toronto, Canada M5C 1P9

A Personal Library publication
produced exclusively for
Thomas Nelson & Sons (Canada) Limited
81 Curlew Drive, Don Mills, Canada
M3A 2R1

Publisher: Glenn Edward Witmer
Editor: Claire Gerus
Designer: Jonathan Milne

Canadian Cataloguing in Publication Data

Teatero, William, 1953-
Mackenzie King

(Canada's Heritage in Pictures)

Includes index.
ISBN 0-17-600740-7

1. King, William Lyon Mackenzie, 1874-1950.
2. Prime ministers – Canada – Biography.
3. Canada – Politics and government – 1911-
I. Title. II. Series.

FC581.K5T43   971.06'22'0924   C79-094155-4
F1033.K53T43

The publisher has made every
effort to give accurate credit to
the sources of quotations and il-
lustrations which appear in this
book. In the event of error or
omission, notification would be
appreciated.

Printed and bound in Canada

Acknowledgments
I would like to thank the staffs of the Public Archives of Canada, photographic collection, the Queen's University Archives, the Public Archives of Ontario, the City of Toronto Archives, particularly Linda Price, the University of Toronto Archives, particularly Bob Taylor-Vaisey and Harold Averill, the United Church Archives in Toronto, and Sandra Guillaume of the Multicultural Historical Society of Ontario. Donald Swainson carefully read the manuscript and I am thankful for his patience and encouragement. I shall always be grateful to Cathy Van Baren for her useful editorial assistance and for the long hours she generously gave in the securing of photographs.

Much of the material in this book has been taken directly from the King diaries, but the author owes a great debt to those excellent and dedicated scholars without whose published sources this work could not have been written.

For Eve,

And to the memory of William Kyle

Preface

Few Canadians ever pretended to like William Lyon Mackenzie King. Sir Wilfrid Laurier had been the "plumed knight," claiming devotion even from those who differed with him. Sir John A. Macdonald's capacity for drawing affection became one of the links that held a fragile young Dominion together. Even Sir Robert Borden's craggy integrity drew associates to him.

Canada would not have lasted an hour on the warmth Mackenzie King could draw from his countrymen. Most Canadians were ashamed of his pompous, banal speeches. In wartime, they yearned for the dramatic leadership of a Roosevelt or a Churchill. After each Liberal election triumph, it was the frequent duty of the party elders to find their prime minister a fresh constituency. Voters might want King's party and his policies; they did not want him.

Canada's tiny corps of intellectuals felt duty-bound to denounce the Liberal leader as if he were the embodiment of all those evasive compromises which they so deplored in Canada. "We had no shape," complained Frank Scott, "because he never took sides, and no sides because he never allowed them to take shape."

Mackenzie King would have squirmed under this complaint as he did under any criticism, yet it was also the summation of his genius. The truth about William Lyon Mackenzie King was that he was, above all, a mediator. His most perceptive biographer, Blair Neatby, recognized King's deepest abiding principle: that reasonable men, meeting around a table, could somehow resolve any problem. King's affliction was that all men were not reasonable. From his first meeting with the workers of Valleyfield and their hard-featured employers to his final struggle against the confrontation of the Cold War, King reserved his deepest disgust for those who could not compromise. His delight was to isolate them, whether they were "ignorant idealists" or "Tory-minded." A good mediator would be prepared to negotiate with the devil himself. Mackenzie King came close when he addressed those letters that began: "Dear Herr Hitler . . ."

The practices of the mediator became the methods of Mackenzie King's politics. Majorities may win, he realized, but minorities must never be humiliated. Like any expert arbitrator, King added steadily to his arsenal of tricks. Every possible advantage must be quietly stored away until it is needed. J.L. Ralston's 1942 resignation might be forgotten, perhaps even by its author. King had it and he used it two and a half years later.

"Blessed are the peacemakers," records the Gospel according to St. Matthew, "because they shall be called the sons of God." In their lifetime, they are called much else. Mediators rarely can be heroes. Part of their art is to leave the limelight for others. The luxuries of non-negotiable demands and immovable principles are not for them.

Western Canadians could hardly be persuaded to celebrate King as the best friend their region had ever had in Ottawa but they did something much more important. They abandoned their protest votes for the Progressives and turned the prairie provinces into a Liberal stronghold. Quebeckers would not pour out their gratitude to King because he had dodged and delayed and compromised over conscription almost until the war was won but they knew him as the best ally they were likely to find.

To contemporaries, King was such a personification of fussy dullness that people came to believe that all Canadian politicians and perhaps even all Canadians were cast in the same dreary mold. This was absurd. The politicians of King's era were men like William Aberhart, Camillien Houde, Mitchell F. Hepburn or James Shaver Woodsworth. What contemporaries did not know was that Mackenzie King was perhaps the most extraordinary of the lot.

How would Canadians have responded if they had known that their drab, corpulent prime minister worshipped his mother, summoned up the spirit of Sir Wilfrid Laurier and William Ewart Gladstone and interpreted each of his life's coincidences as a divine message? Because King's executors ignored his express wish that his massive private diaries should be destroyed, Canada's least-known prime minister has become our most exposed. No public figure anywhere has left such a detailed record of his thoughts and emotions. Even Sam Pepys would

have blushed to transcribe the thoughts that King painstakingly preserved for posterity. In a country starved of three-dimensional characters, King's private life and fantasies can now fuel every imaginable interpretation.

All of this makes Mackenzie King a more interesting and compassionate figure than his own age would ever have guessed. Yet surprisingly little of this really mattered to the history of Canada.

It would be fun to pretend that Mackenzie King governed the country with his crystal ball and his table-rapping. The truth is that he did not. His spiritualism was a hobby. When, infrequently, he drew on the spirit world for political prophecies, he was almost invariably deceived. In office, insists Charles Stacey, King was too busy to find more than occasional consolation in that "very double life" he led.

For Canada, that life had enormous significance. We know now that Sir Wilfrid Laurier never claimed that the Twentieth Century would belong to Canada though that myth is unlikely ever to be eradicated. However, between them Laurier and King ensured that Canada would belong to the Liberal Party. Of the two, King's contribution was

both longer and more successful. Laurier's career ended in a shattered party and the divided Canada of 1917. King could retire when he chose, leaving his party almost a decade of power on the impetus he had given it.

King wanted always to be more than a mediator and a politician. Driven by his upbringing and his academic credentials to appear more than an agile opportunist, he struggled to furnish his mind with philosophical principles. One result was that tedious volume, *Industry and Humanity;* another was that series of secular sermons with which he bored audiences, cabinet colleagues and the House of Commons. King took enormous pains over their composition and immense pride in their delivery. They remain, unlike his diaries, stubbornly unreadable.

Time has not improved King's claim on the affections of Canadians. The diaries make him pathetic without being tragic. However, King, the politician, has grown steadily. Even some of the intellectuals who so detested him – Frank Underhill, Eugene Forsey, Bernard Ostry – became faithful servants of his Liberal Party.

Since Mackenzie King, Canada has experienced

other forms of prime ministerial leadership. The country has survived "visions" and outlived "charisma" – but only barely. Perhaps too late we have learned to value a political leader who:
   ...skilfully avoided what was wrong Without saying what was right, And never let his on the one hand Know what his on the other hand was doing.
Our politicians tell us that Canada has become a very difficult country to govern. It never was anything else. What our contemporary leaders have forgotten is the capacity to mediate and a capacity to see a little beyond each crisis. They could find no better instructor than the strange, introverted figure who managed Canada longer than any other man and who left it stronger and more united than any of his successors.

If this book helps Canadians to understand the achievement of Mackenzie King, it will have served a great national purpose.

Desmond Morton
March 27th, 1979
Mississauga

7

Introduction

On Dominion day, 1934, Mackenzie King, then leader of the Opposition, returned from a gruelling day's work to his Kingsmere cottage. He reached it just before dawn. As he walked across his lawn in the moonlight "...suddenly there came over me, as if bursting upon me – the meaning of it all." It was a sense of returning. "It was 'home' at last, the end of the journey from the past to the future ... I am where I was in Woodside days, in college days, in early days at Ottawa with the desire for service and duty as a guide." He felt the reassuring presence of the spirit world guiding him, as it had always done, on that significant day. "As I reflected upon everything that was happening, I began to see very clearly that ... dear father and others [i.e. beyond the grave] were helping me to get back to those days."

King believed the truths of the spirit world, or God's divine plan, could be revealed through daily occurrences, and he observed a moral truth in every event, no matter how complicated or petty. But if King was a mystic, he was also utilitarian, and for him a practical spirit world revealed its purpose for his benefit through coincidences, numerology and direct contact. After a séance in 1934, he wrote, "There was a feeling of reality about the invisible which seemed to clothe me with a sense of power."

The relation between Mackenzie King's spiritual beliefs and his success as a politician has never been clear. Certainly he believed the two were inseparable. But King operated in a very real, political world. Through sheer tenacity and political savvy (he had no charisma), he held power longer than any other politician in Canadian history. Mediums who "worked" for him during his years as prime minister were quick to point out after his death that he did not rely on the spirits to make policy decisions. They merely reassured him about decisions already made, and advised him on private affairs. Similarly, his preoccupation with numerology and his obsession for coincidences seems never to have interfered with his political decision-making. The spirit world provided him with his energy and his mission.

The relationship between King's peculiar character and his political success is far more subtle. If his source of energy was unusual, his style of leadership bewildered both his contemporaries and historians. The art of politics lies in the successful balancing of conflicting interests. In Canada, the ability to forge new consensus in a changing society while achieving harmony between the French and English populations – which constitute our deepest potential division – has been the measure of our politicians. In this art King, like Macdonald and Laurier, was consummate. He continued the historic pattern of French-English cooperation through a national party, at the same time proving sensitive to other interests and regions in the country. His consensus-oriented, cautious approach was the key to his success. King aggravated our differences least.

The major criticism of Mackenzie King's style is that if he did not divide us, neither did he inspire a positive unity. He was moralistic but vague, and often avoided and confused issues. He was colourless and to many Canadians did not convey a national vision. King seemed to lead by reminding us of our divisions, and thus, our potential for disintegration.

Yet the nearly 22 years of King's prime ministership were difficult years in which to govern, and King, with or without a positive platform, did hold Canadians together. Canada was transformed into a major industrial power; a new sense of national identity was fostered and nurtured by nationalistic artists and intellectuals; Canada's sovereignty was recognized throughout the world; and government control over her economy and the shape of her society became the rule. King had governed Canada from "model 'T'" to television, from family enterprise to multinational corporations, from unrestricted capitalism to massive government intervention.

Through all this King was fatalistic. All was unfolding as the spirits assured him it should. As long as he was prime minister and the Liberal party was in power, God's will would be done in Canada, and his mission accomplished. The spirits did not govern the country, but they provided Canada's most enigmatic leader with a mission.

It is true that King was not a great leader, despite the divine source from which his mission was secured, but he was successful because he was content to be, and to make the Liberal party, a mirror for all Canadians.

William Teatero
March 12, 1979
Toronto

Laurier House was in blackness.

A stream of moonlight filtered through the windows revealing three figures – among them the aging leader of the Liberal party – huddled around a small table. An old, white-haired woman reached for a silver trumpet and brought it to her lips. The voices of the "dead" droned ominously through it, eerie sounds echoing through the large, empty house. The message ended.

Who was this politician seeking reassurance from the spirit world?

His name was Mackenzie King, and he would hold the office of prime minister longer than any other Canadian politician.

From his childhood, Mackenzie King had felt a sense of mission.

His mother, to whom he was devoted, told him of her sufferings as the daughter of William Lyon Mackenzie. Her father's rebellion against the Upper Canadian Tories had been thwarted, and he had been exiled as a traitor. Subtly but permanently, she bestowed on her son the mission of restoring honour to the family name.

Near the end of his life he wrote, "My prayer to be a medium of expressing the will of God on earth has been answered, and inspiration has come to me from those who have gone but continue to work from the Beyond in the saving of men and nations."

King became convinced, through his mystical Calvinist upbringing, that his destiny was predetermined. But to fulfill his destiny he would eventually need the support and guidance of those beyond the grave.

Painting of Mackenzie King's mother by J.W.L. Forster

The sense of mission began here.

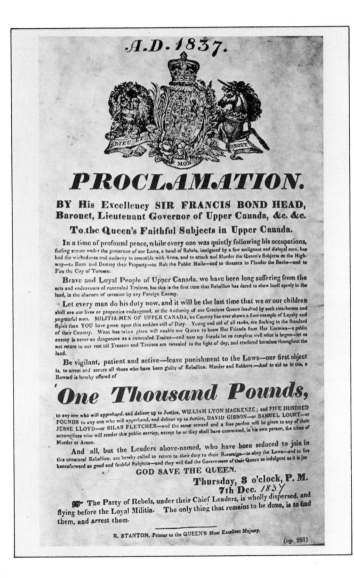

King's grandfather, William Lyon Mackenzie, was born in 1795 and grew up fatherless in the highlands of Scotland. He, too, was imbued with a sense of mission by a domineering mother.

Reward poster for W.L. Mackenzie, outlaw

He grew up to be a famous Canadian rebel.

William Lyon Mackenzie's printing office, corner of Front and Frederick Streets in Toronto

As editor of the radical Toronto newspaper, *The Constitution*, Mackenzie planned a general uprising across Upper Canada to free aggrieved farmers from the yoke of Tory rule. In early December, 1837, he urged his followers to march to Toronto and overthrow the government. Neighbour told neighbour and settlers throughout northern Toronto's farm country began to organize and drill.

The mismanaged marchers damaged private property and seized a mail coach before being routed by the government supporters. Mackenzie escaped to the U.S. where poverty and family illness made his life in exile miserable.

In later years, having failed to establish his vision in Upper Canada, he considered himself a voice in the wilderness, decrying alone the sins of Canadian politics. He would remain, for some, a martyr to the cause of political liberty; for others, he was a damned traitor.

Mackenzie's thirteenth child, Isabel Grace, was born in poverty and exile, February 6, 1843.

The youngest of the rebel's children, she felt deeply the taint of her father's treason. On her return to Toronto in 1850 from the U.S., she sought acceptance from her new community. More than that, she wished to see vindicated her father's mission to rescue Canadian society from the grip of the Tories.

She also hoped he would one day be recognized as a national hero.

In 1872 Isabel married John King, a young lawyer with scholarly ambitions.

A popular speaker, King contributed regularly to newspapers and periodicals in Berlin, Ontario, and Toronto. He was not, however, a successful lawyer, and in 1893 accepted a position as part-time lecturer at Osgoode Hall, the Law School of Upper Canada. He held this position for twenty-two years.

King was deeply devoted to his family, quick to praise his children for their virtues, and willing to sacrifice for their happiness.

They had four children.

Isabel Christina Grace (Bella) was followed by William Lyon Mackenzie (Willie), Janet Lindsey (Jennie), and Dougall Macdougall (Max or Mac).

Mrs. King did not live in an age – nor did she possess the talents – to bring honour to her father's name. She therefore chose to use her influence on her first-born son.

A favourite pose, Willie overlooking the family

The Kings settled in Berlin (now Kitchener), Ontario.

The happiest of their four Berlin homes was "Woodside" where, between 1886 and 1893, they raised their family.

Woodside, with its wild flowers, small orchard, farm animals, and large shady trees, was the site of all the children's summer ramblings. Music and theatrics were favourite family pastimes as were walks in the woods. In the evening they would gather around for a sing-song, with papa on the castanents and mother, always the centre of attention, playing the piano.

At an early age, Willie was singled out as special by his mother.

Bella and Jennie King in cavalier costumes

Young Willie King was imbued with all the energy of his fiery rebel grandfather. His determined mother told him solemnly that there was a score to settle on her family's behalf.

William Lyon Mackenzie King carried the burden of his grandfather's name along with his mother's hopes that he would re-establish the name "Mackenzie" with honour and fortune.

From his earliest youth, Mackenzie King was alive with anxiety to fulfill this mission. Why had he inherited the name of his grandfather, he wondered? "Surely," he wrote, "I have some great work to accomplish before I die."

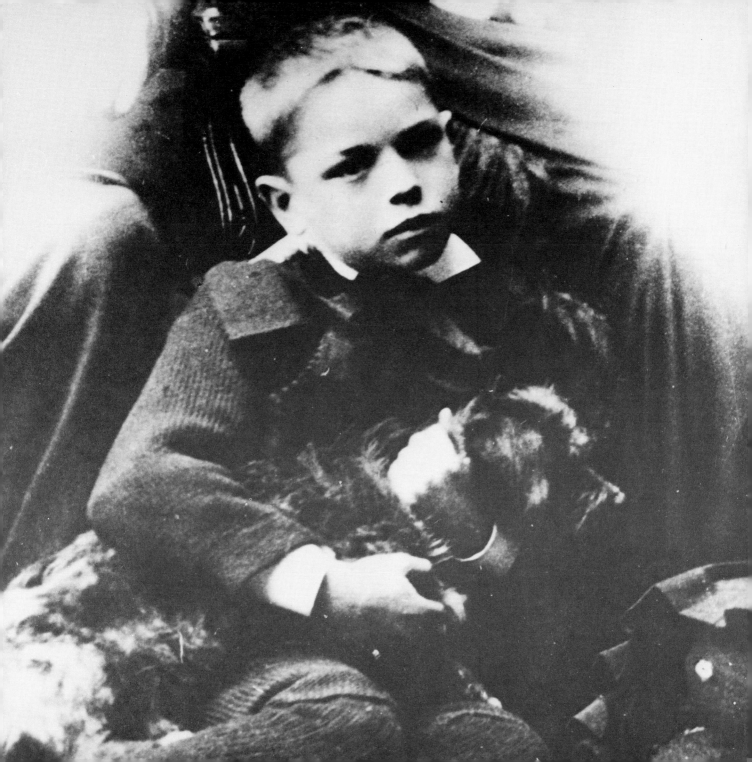

Willie's father was an active supporter of the Liberal party, and young Willie was exposed to politics early in life. In 1882, at the age of seven, he was taken to hear a speech by Sir John A. Macdonald. King later recalled how he was caught up in the enthusiasm.

"I remember best not the political argument, but that Sir John was presented with some flowers by a pretty young lady whom he thanked with an embrace. I could do nothing but envy him, and decided then that politics had its rewards."

Could politics be the path that would lead to pleasing his mother?

At sixteen, Willie took his first steps toward independence. He left Woodside and the security of his happy childhood. Here, his mother would await the successful achievement of his mission.

She did not direct his career; she had no clear idea of how he would distinguish himself. But she transferred to her son an undirected energy and profound sense of family loyalty that galvanized his own sense of mission.

At 17, King entered the University of Toronto.

University College after the fire of
February 14, 1890

University College had just been rebuilt following a fire in 1890. Internal changes were taking place as well. For the first time, natural and social sciences were eclipsing the classics in importance, and students were beginning to concern themselves with broader social issues.

In 1888, a department of political science had been formed to offer students practical training in economic and political philosophy. These areas were deemed increasingly important for Canada as a growing industrial nation.

He was a serious student, but there were lighter moments, too.

Willie indulged in occasional forays to the nearby girls' schools, where exuberant undergraduates would sing, to the chagrin of shocked Torontonians.

King, nicknamed "Rex" by his colleagues, also participated in one or two parties that escalated into riots. On Hallowe'en, 1893, he and five comrades tore down an old shed on campus. Each was fined $15 for boisterousness.

More serious disruptions, however, were in store for the university.

King's friends tended to be of the teetotaling variety, generally dedicated, idealistic young men

Strike!

On February 18, 1895, the corridors of University College were alive with student activity, but the classrooms were empty. The students, led by the editorial staff of their newspaper, *The Varsity*, were on strike. They had charged the administration with corruption and nepotism in choosing its staff.

King was not one of the leaders.

He did not possess the charisma of T. Hamar Greenwood of the Political Science Club, who later became Viscount Greenwood, a British cabinet minister. Nor did he display the integrity of *The Varsity* editor James Tucker, later to become editor of *Saturday Night*, who faced expulsion from the university for his virulent editorial.

The Varsity

TORONTO, *February 13th, 1895.*

Published weekly by the Students of the University of Toronto. Annual subscription, $1. For advertising rates apply to the Chairman of the Business Board. Address all communications for publication to the Editor-in-Chief.

JAS. A. TUCKER, Editor-in-Chief.
EDWARD GILLIS, Chairman of Business Board.

Business Board.—Miss Fraser,'95 ; W. A. MacKinnon, 97 ; C. W. Macpherson, School of Practical Science ; W. Thom, '95, W. H. Libby, '98, Medicine.

Editorial Board.—J. Montgomery, '95 ; J. R. Perry, '96 ; Miss E. Durand, '95 ; W. Shotwell, '97 ; V. G. Smith, School of Practical Science ; E. T. Kellam, '95, H. L. Heath, '97, Medicine.

Assistant Editors.—J. L. Murray, '95 ; C. P. Megan, 95 ; W. B. Hendry, '95 ; H. A. Clark, '95 ; W. L. M. King, '95 ; P. J. Robinson, '96 ; A. R. Clute, '96 ; C. H. Clegg, '97.

" Suffer yourself to be blamed, imprisoned, condemned ; suffer yourself to be hanged ; but publish your opinions ; it is not a right, it is a duty."

"Here, in this year of grace 1895, we behold the University torn by dissension – rent in twain by the fatuous policy of selfish, small-minded men."
The Varsity, University of Toronto

King was, however, convinced of the validity of the students' cause. In an address to an assembly of undergraduates, he urged a student boycott of classes until a royal commission could enquire into the university administration. The motion passed unanimously.

An offer by University of Toronto President Loudon to meet with students to discuss grievances appeased King, who then favoured calling off the strike. But the students got their royal commission, and finally settled back into their books – all except James Tucker, who was expelled.

Rex" King studied for long hours, cloistered in his room and at the university library.

The long hours brought their rewards. King was academically outstanding. But he was haunted by his mission and the terror of failure. He drove himself to excess, and despite his early academic success, was never completely satisfied with himself.

Other students recognized that he was already "practising" for a higher office as he became a member of the Political Science Club and an assistant editor for *The Varsity*.

He enjoyed conventional activities – dances, debates and athletics – but found himself irresistibly drawn to the decadence and suffering beyond the university's sheltering walls.

Toronto the Good.

Toronto was a growing industrial-commercial city (population 181,000) when Mackenzie King arrived in 1891. Considered a "moral" place, it was known as "Toronto the Good."

But Toronto was not so good. In 1898, C.S. Clark published a social study of the city which exposed its corruption, gambling houses, prostitution, shocking poverty, pickpockets, swindlers, drunkenness, and social diseases.

King struggled with the city's temptations.

"You meet a girl on the street and a flash from her eyes will tell you what she is. You look back after passing her, and she does the same. If you desire to follow her, do so, and the probabilities are 99 to 1 that you have a street-walker." – *C.S. Clark, speaking of Toronto in 1898.*

"There is no doubt I lead a very double life. I strive to do right and continually do wrong...I fear I am much like Peter, I deny my Lord when the maid smiles at me, but with God's help I will overcome even this temptation." – *Mackenzie King, 1898*

King decided to "save" prostitutes from a life of evil.

King Street, Toronto

While a third-year honours student, King launched a personal campaign to raise up these ruined women from the depths of their depravity.

One unfortunate girl who earned her living by soliciting on King Street was stopped in her tracks by young Rex King who implored her "to stop her wicked life and turn to Christ." She paid him no heed. Two days later he presented her with a 50-cent Bible, and she agreed to repent.

Soon, however, she was back at work. King persisted and recorded in his diary: "after playing detective for a while I found she was in [a client's] room but she got out a back way before I could find her. I went down again however and got her; she came back with me."

By the time he graduated, Mackenzie King's "aura of destiny" had been recognized by others.

The class of '95

The intense, ambitious young graduate was, however, racked with indecision and doubt about his future. His unselfish desire to serve God and man was matched by a strong need for personal success. Grandfather and mother provided him with the zeal, but what was to be the form of his mission? The church? Politics? Academics?

King wanted to do graduate work in political economy and sociology at the University of Chicago, but his mother wished him to stay in Toronto and his father wanted him to study law. He decided to remain in Toronto and postpone graduate studies for a year.

In the spring of 1895, he received his Bachelor of Arts degree. B.K. Sandwell, a fellow student who later became a prominent journalist, observed in retrospect: "There were several much more brilliant personages than King in the student body at the time. About King, however, there hung already a sort of aura of destiny, which to me was inexplicable by anything in his personality or performance, and which probably emanated from his own absolute conviction that he had what in religious circles is designated a 'call'."

"I will find this a good plan —
to see the shadowy side of life."

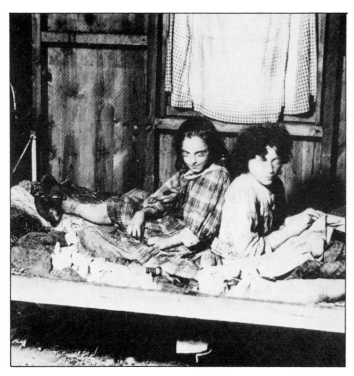

In the summer of 1895, Willie King began work as a journalist, first at the Toronto *News*, then at the Toronto *Globe*. In the evenings his father supervised him while he read law. This daily work involved reporting on the police court proceedings, a task that enabled him to see firsthand the grim side of the city.

By the fall of 1896, although not yet 22 years old, King had an honours B.A. with a first class standing, a law degree, and a year's experience as a journalist.

The misery and wretchedness were too much for him.

His mission took him to the University of Chicago for a graduate degree and active participation in the settlement work of a famous social worker, Jane Addams, at Hull House.

Less than two months later, he left Hull House. Although he greatly admired Jane Addams and her work, he did not have the stomach for live-in social work. After receiving his M.A. in the spring of 1897, he left Chicago and undertook another arduous task – obtaining a fellowship in economics at the University of Toronto.

Because of their dedication to humanitarian service, nurses had always held a special fascination for King.

Baby ward, Hospital for Sick
Children, Toronto

As a university student
he had regularly con-
ducted religious services
at Toronto's Hospital for
Sick Children. Many of the
nurses he befriended be-
came long-time friends.

While a graduate student in Chicago, he became ill and in the spring of 1897 spent time in a Chicago hospital. Here he met nurse Mathilde Grossert, with whom he would fall in love.

His life was thrown into chaos.

Although occupied with applying for fellowships at Harvard and the University of Toronto, he found himself obsessed with thoughts of Nurse Grossert. He disciplined himself not to go back to Chicago, but released his feelings through impassioned letters to her.

But the problems of others also claimed his attention.

To help finance his education King researched and published four articles on Toronto's social problems for the *Mail and Empire*. The response was strong. Torontonians were shocked by King's descriptions of the exploitation of labour in the garment industry.

Women worked from dawn to dusk for only a few cents an hour, while profits were high for contractors and sub-contractors. Immigrant children were often used as a source of cheap labour.

In the course of his investigations, King discovered that federal government contracts to produce letter carriers' uniforms had gone to some of the worst sweatshops. He was sensitive to the potential embarrassment this would bring the Liberals if revealed in the Conservative *Mail and Empire*. Instead, he and his father paid a visit to the Hon. William Mulock, then Postmaster General.

Mulock, a Liberal friend of Willie's father, was impressed by the young man's concern.

He commissioned King to further investigate on behalf of the Canadian government the sweating of labour in Toronto, Montreal, and Hamilton.

King's report to the Postmaster General focused on working conditions in the manufacture of uniforms for the Canadian Post Office, the Militia and the North West Mounted Police. Many of his recommendations were later embodied in the Fair Wages Resolution, passed in 1900, which called for the elimination of subcontracting and the establishment of fair wage rates for all government contracts.

King had made an invaluable contact, and had been identified as a friend of labour.

Mulock and Laurier

King was accepted at Harvard for graduate study.

Alone in his room, far from home, his loneliness worked relentlessly upon him. As he struggled with his political studies, he found his thoughts turning to love and his Chicago nurse.

He poured all his feelings for her into letters that portended a marriage. With her at his side, he wrote in his diary, he would carry on Grandfather Mackenzie's fight; she would share in his destiny. For her love he would struggle with the Devil himself.

"There is this very night," his diary records on March 31, 1898, "the eternal fight within my breast. Sin and wrong

would tear her from me. Thoughts come to me which are begotten of the devil...you offer me ambition and the world. You tell me to gain it alone – to hell again with you all. For in my best, my purest moments I love this woman most."

Had he forgotten the mission?

His mother wrote to him upon hearing of his matrimonial plans: "I have built castles without number for you. Are all these dreams but to end in dreams? I am getting old now Willie and disappointment wearies and the heart grows sick."

In his diary he confided: "The world is fighting hard to keep Miss Grossert from me but I know my heart...and it will be hard to meet the world alone."

He travelled to Toronto in April, plagued by nightmares and fitful sleep. "I never saw father and mother look so careworn and distressed in all my life," he wrote of their meeting.

King finally submitted to pressures from home and his own indecision.

Mathilde Grossert eventually married George Edward Barchet. Here, she is shown with her year-old daughter, Stephanie.

He recorded the essence of his discussions with his family in his diary: "I am told I will spoil all my chances in life." He felt, however, that he was becoming more ambitious, materialistic, and selfish. God had given him Mathilde in order that he might overcome his moral indifference. His parents did not buy this argument; he had other responsibilities. "Then I was told I am neglectful of those I love at home, unkind, untrue to them . . . it is the hardest part for me to bear. Was it right for father and mother to ask me to break off this love?"

The stress numbed him. He felt "no emotion, all indifference, cold and hard," and in this frame of mind he went to Chicago to talk to Mathilde.

"I have kept faith with those at home, with Mathilde and myself," he wrote after seeing her and agreeing to postpone the engagement, but back in New England he kissed her photo and sank deep into anguished depression.

When he thought of his beloved nurse, the pain was unbearable. And when he thought of his mother . . ."Why was I not always with mother? I should have shown more love to her. If God spares her and me may he give me strength to prove my love."

That summer he again travelled to Chicago to see Mathilde; two days before leaving he wrote: " . . . she is more to me like a mother than a sweetheart . . ." and there was only room for one mother in his life. When he returned it was over between them.

From then on King dedicated himself to rising in the world.

He lived alone to better control his time and methods of study. Besides, he discovered, "you can better control people if you don't see too much of them." He began to distinguish himself at Harvard.

His expression of love for his mother grew steadily and remarkably. He kept five photographs of her, and never missed an opportunity to lavish her with affection.

In September, 1899, King set sail for Europe.

Harvard renewed his fellowship, and King went abroad for a year to study current industrial problems. He stayed for a time in a London settlement house, and attended meetings of the Fabian Socialist Society.

But King was never a socialist. He favoured the existing system of private ownership of industry, and believed that state regulation could correct the abuses of industrialized society.

He read, travelled, discussed and lectured on labour relations.

King was becoming an expert on questions of labour.

His timing was perfect. Canada was just entering a period of growth and industrial expansion that would transform the nation between 1896 and 1914. Canadians were vitally interested in the issues of industrial labour, wages, collective bargaining, strikes, labour legislation and the role of labour in modern society.

In the spring of 1900, the Laurier administration formed a Department of Labour, with William Mulock in charge. In June, Mulock wired King in Rome, offering him the position of deputy minister and the editorship of the department's new publication, the *Labour Gazette*. King accepted, and in July, 1900, sailed home to Canada.

Public works employees at the turn of the century

Meanwhile, three important political contemporaries were making the news, all of whom would loom large in King's destiny.

Sir Wilfrid Laurier had just been elected to his second term as prime minister of Canada.

Young Winston Churchill (King's age) had recently made an heroic escape from war-engulfed South Africa, and was now in the first year of his lengthy career in British Parliament.

John D. Rockefeller was a major American industrialist.

In 1901 King told his mother what he believed his destiny would be.

"I kept my arm around her, and as I looked at the side of her face, with her forehead bare to the cold breeze, her white curl and hair flowing behind...I could see the strongest resemblance to grandfather, and I thought of him as he must have toured this country in election and rebellion times ...partly to express my own ambition and partly because my soul was large, my spirit strong and resolve great, I whispered to mother that I believed, that if opportunity came in the future I might become the Premier of this country...If I ever do, or come near to such a mark, it will be due to her life and love that I have done so."

King with his mother

For the next seven years the young deputy minister worked hard to gain the attention of Prime Minister Wilfrid Laurier.

King worked long hours in "gloomy Ottawa", expanding the Department of Labour and preparing legislation on labour questions.

He also acted as a mediator in industrial disputes, as a royal commissioner investigating problems of labour and immigration, and as a representative of the government to other nations in matters affecting immigration and labour.

Even his social life became a tool for advancement.

He wrote his parents about his social climbing. "I think I told you I was at dinner at Government House not long ago and took in Mrs. Hanbury-Williams [the wife of the Governor-General's private secretary]. I was also at dinner at Sir Louis Davies' [Judge of the Supreme Court of Canada] with Sir Wilfrid and Lady Laurier and others and at a luncheon at the golf club given by Mr. Fisher [the Minister of Agriculture], sat next to Lady Laurier. Mrs. Willard (wife of the Govr. of Virginia) was another guest, about 10 altogether. Was at dinner at Mr. Hyman's [Minister of Public Works] a night or two ago."

King's only close friend was H.A. Harper.

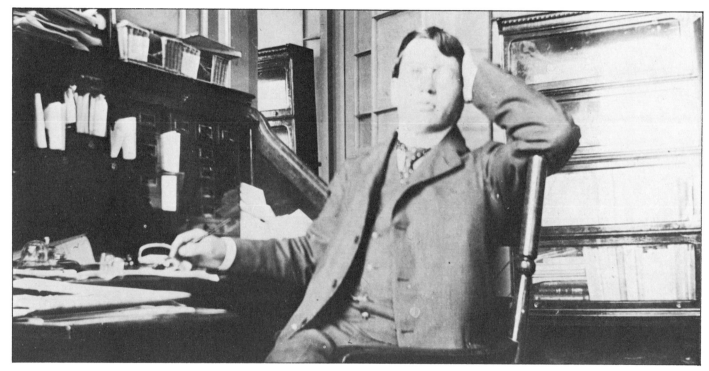

"Bert" Harper was a friend and fellow member of the class of '95. He had been the Ottawa correspondent for the Montreal *Herald* when King arrived in Ottawa. They took rooms together and by October, 1900, Harper was Associate Editor of the *Labour Gazette*.

King and Harper shared the same ideals and interests. They worked enthusiastically for the advancement of the working classes. In their leisure time, they read poetry aloud to each other and spent weekends together on nature hikes.

But grief was to come to King through this friendship.

On December 6, 1901, King was in British Columbia attempting to mediate a labour dispute. Back in Ottawa, Bert went skating with a group of friends. A young woman skated through soft ice into the deep, fast Ottawa River, and Harper jumped in to save her. Both were drowned.

To commemorate this act of heroism, a monument was erected by the citizens of Ottawa on Wellington Street in front of the Parliament buildings. King was a member of the committee appointed to supervise the project, and the choice of Galahad was apparently his.

King (second from left) at the unveiling of a statue honouring Harper's heroism.

King, desolate, again plunged into his work.

He now focused on winning a cabinet position. His reputation as a labour trouble-shooter soon brought him a new opportunity to gain recognition.

Labour groups were just beginning to organize, and industrialists were slow to recognize them. They preferred to deal with workers individually, especially where cheap, unorganized immigrant labour was plentiful.

In 1907, unionized labour in British Columbia formed the Anti-Asiatic League. They hoped to lobby the federal government into limiting Asian immigration. In September, rioting broke out and property was damaged in the Chinese and Japanese sections of Vancouver.

Damage incurred during the anti-Asiatic riots in Vancouver, B.C., September 8-9, 1907

The federal government appointed Mackenzie King, a royal commission of one, to investigate.

King concluded that the government must take strong steps to protect "higher standards of labour." He recommended excluding further Asian competition in the Canadian labour market. As a result, the Canadian government negotiated an agreement with the imperial Japanese government which severely limited Japanese emigration to Canada.

King also persuaded the Indian government to enforce a clause in the Indian Emigration Act prohibiting Indians from leaving the country under contract to work in Canada. Since few Indians would want to leave India for Canada without having already secured work, they were practically, if not technically, excluded from immigrating to Canada.

"The 20th century belongs to Canada."

In 1908, Sir Wilfrid had been prime minister for 12 years. During his premiership the nation had been transformed from the weak sister in North America to a vibrant, confident nation. She was eager to develop her resources in field, forest, fishery and mine.

World trade revived, and there was an increased demand for Canadian wheat. The West was a "new land," and as the population swelled the Canadian prairies became the "breadbasket of Europe."

Business was booming. Canadian banks in Toronto and Montreal were rising faster and higher

than church steeples, and Canadians enjoyed nearly full employment. Everywhere, progress and optimism abounded. The boast that the 20th century belonged to Canada was affirmed. Laurier, although he may never have spoken the famous words, certainly agreed with the senti-ment. He told Canadians: "In 1908 Canada has become a star to which is directed the gaze of the whole civilized world," and he determined to fight an election on his government's record.

In September, 1908, King was named the Liberal candidate for North Waterloo, Ontario.

King had strong support from the many friends and contacts he had developed during his eight years as deputy minister of labour. The greatest help came from the influential Toronto *Globe*, which spared no effort in seeking his election. King was referred to as "the brilliant young adminis-trator," and was considered excellent cabinet material. Even Sir Wilfrid Laurier spoke on his behalf in Berlin, Ontario in September.

King's opponent was Richard Reid, the Conservative candidate for North Waterloo. Reid's campaign manager was Alexander Wright. The Liberal newspaper, the Berlin *Daily Telegram*, retorted: "King can do more than Reid and Wright in Ottawa."

Laurier campaigning for King (left, seated)

The young Liberal had something for everyone.

He presented himself as a friend to labour, and his record as deputy minister confirmed that he was willing to bring in legislation favourable to the workers. Meanwhile he told businessmen that his moderate and conciliatory approach to labour disputes would bring improved industrial relations, and thus increased productivity and prosperity.

61

At 33 he was elected member of parliament; at 34 he was named minister of labour.

His parents watched from the gallery as the prime minister introduced him to the Commons. King thought of his mother: "...there is reward in this for her as well as me, reward for the sacrifices her father made, and for what she has had to make in consequence. If her father could only have been present too...He would have felt a recompense for all his struggle."

King with his parents

In 1908 King had the opportunity to preserve the sacred memory of his grandfather's cause. William Dawson LeSueur, who had been commissioned to write the biography of William Lyon Mackenzie for the major Canadian history series, *The Makers of Canada*, submitted his manuscript to George Morang for publication. It was an unsympathetic biography, and Willie and his friends pressured Morang into refusing to publish it. Then began a four-year-long court struggle between George Lindsey (King's cousin) and the author, for possession of the manuscript.

In 1912, the courts ruled that LeSueur had fraudulently obtained access to Mackenzie's papers, after allegedly promising to produce a sympathetic biography. The manuscript was seized by Lindsey, and Willie, who had been in court every day, was relieved. Grandfather's image was still safe.

For the next two years Mackenzie King was minister of labour.

During this brief period his ministry proposed an eight-hour work day for the civil service, made provision for more comprehensive accumulation of statistics relating to labour, and introduced a plan of compensation for injured workers.

But by 1911, although King was energetic and efficient, his party was old and tired.

Sir Wilfrid had been confident that his proposal for reciprocal lower trade tariffs with the United States would win him the election. "Surely the Lord is good unto his own, for He has delivered mine enemies into mine hands," he said when the Conservatives opposed reciprocity. But after 15 years in power his enemies were strong enough to overpower his weary, stale and arrogant government.

Two sensitive issues led to his downfall.

Overseas, the British navy had been struggling to keep up with German naval expansion. In answer to his opposition's call for a direct contribution to the British navy, Laurier proposed the creation of a Canadian navy.

In Quebec, his proposals were treated as an unwarranted concession to British imperialism. Many English-speaking Canadians, however, considered it a grossly inadequate contribution to imperial defence. A Canadian navy, they felt, could never be anything but "tin-pot."

Canadians turned their backs on Laurier.

He was depicted as selling Canada down the river to the Yankees while handing it back to the British on a "tin pot" platter. Sadly he reflected, "I am branded in Quebec as a traitor to the French, and in Ontario as a traitor to the English. In Quebec I am branded as a Jingo, and in Ontario as a Separatist...I am neither. I am a Canadian...I have held before me as a pillar of fire by night and a pillar of cloud by day a policy of true Canadianism, of moderation, of conciliation."

Laurier addressing a Montreal gathering

Like most Liberals in 1911, King went down to defeat.

The Conservative government of Robert Laird Borden was now at the helm. Borden, a prosperous and talented Halifax lawyer, brought with him the support of Canadian business. Although he formed a competent and able administration that would bring credit to Canada in the first world war, he did not have the support of, nor did he understand, French Canada. This weakness was to loom large before the war was over.

King was temporarily forced to seek an alternate career.

For the next three years, he survived by working for the Liberal party and by writing occasional newspaper articles. He was saved from financial worry by an idealistic and wealthy young woman.

Miss Violet Markham had met King in Ottawa during her tour of Canadian industry. An Englishwoman of deep convictions, she was impressed with his work and shared his enthusiasm for social and industrial reform. She contributed to his election campaign in 1911, and hearing of his defeat, wrote to him:

"The simple fact is that I want to help you at this crisis, for Canada's sake as fully as your own. For the next three years I want you to take from me £300 a year so that your hands may be free and your independence assured through this time of crisis. There is nothing in such a gift which may not be offered by me and accepted by you in most perfect simplicity ... So dear Rex for three years feel you are free to work and rest, to lie fallow and study and read and think, without your life being obsessed by the trespassing cares of daily bread."

The money was most welcome, and King and Miss Markham continued to be friends until King's death.

Miss Violet Markham

King did not enjoy being idle, and was anxious to get back into politics.

Suddenly, the guns of August, 1914, shattered the ominous calm of Western Europe.

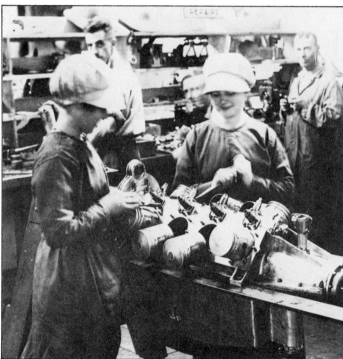

When Great Britain declared war on Germany on August 4, 1914, she did so for all the king's Dominions, and Canada immediately began preparing for war.

The Great War would
change the course of
civilization.

It would be more brutal,
more demanding and
more total than anyone
imagined in 1914.

Within six weeks peaceful Canadian citizens...

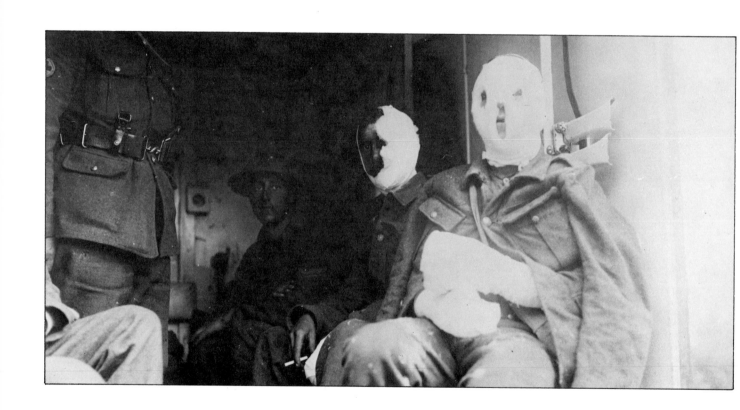

...found themselves fighting in the trenches and foxholes of Europe.

Meanwhile, Mackenzie King was fighting a war of a different kind.

In 1907, while still a deputy minister, he had invited Harvard President C.W. Eliot to speak to the Canadian Club in Ottawa. Eliot was interested in the Industrial Disputes Investigation Bill, which King had just prepared for Parliament, and the two began to correspond on matters relating to labour and industry.

In 1914 Eliot, a trustee of the wealthy Rockefeller Foundation, recommended King to John D. Rockefeller Jr. as an expert in labour relations. In June, 1914, King was asked to head the foundation's new Department of Industrial Relations. In return he would be paid the princely (in those days) salary of $12,000 per annum. King accepted, but retained his Canadian citizenship.

He still hoped to stand for election in the next federal election; he had already been nominated in the constituency of North York, Ontario. Retaining Ottawa as his personal base of operations, he enlisted with Rockefeller.

Coal miners in Colorado, 3,000 feet underground

New challenges awaited King as Rockefeller's trouble-shooter.

His first task was to investigate the Rockefellers' uneasy relations with their miners in Colorado.

This was no easy task. Earlier that year, three miners and one youth had been shot to death by the Colorado state militia. Eleven children and two women had also been killed when the militia set fire to a tent colony occupied by striking workers of Rockefellers' Colorado Fuel and Iron Company.

A Colorado Fuel and Iron company town

Hundreds of Colorado families risked starvation to break the Company's stranglehold on their lives. Rockefeller needed advice.

Mackenzie King with John D. Rockefeller

The miners wanted decent pay, elections of the check-weighmen who frequently cheated them, the right to deal at their own stores, to choose their own boarding houses and doctors — to be free from the Company's control of their lives. The first step to that end, they believed, was to have Rockefeller recognize the United Mine Workers Union. This he would not do.

Perhaps a compromise could be found.

King recommended that the miners be granted collective bargaining, but on a company basis. Thus, Rockefeller would not have to recognize the United Mine Workers, but could deal instead with a company union.

Rockefeller accepted the compromise with little difficulty; he liked King and trusted him completely. King warned the industrial baron that "there appeared no alternative so far as he was concerned, to his [Rockefeller's] being either the storm centre of a great revolution in this country or the man who by his fearless stand and position would transfuse a new spirit into industry."

Convincing the miners to accept company unionism would be more difficult.

Mother Jones, an 83-year-old union agitator whom King finally convinced of Rockefeller's sincerity

King met with the miners' representatives in New York in January 1915; he worked hard to gain their approval but failed. Not until leaders of the United Mine Workers had been jailed for "strike crimes" in the spring of 1915, was King successful in gaining the miners' acceptance of his plan.

To improve public and industrial relations, John D. Rockefeller joined King on a trip to Colorado.

A cheerful King with Rockefeller in Denver

The trip was a success.

The two men talked and ate with the miners. They visited their Company-owned homes and school-houses and inspected the mines. Rockefeller even danced with the miners' wives.

King now had the support, trust and friendship of one of the wealthiest and most powerful men in the world. His name was now familiar to North America's top industrialists. King had moved one step closer to the prime minister's office.

Meanwhile, King's fellow Canadians continued to make sacrifices for the war effort.

Prime Minister Borden (second from left)

From Vimy Ridge and Passchendaeles came a new Canadian nationalism. But it was born of slaughter and sacrifice. The Canadian army corps sent 600,000 men to Europe. Over 60,000 of them would never return. Even more would be demanded of Canadians. The cost of war was higher than death.

As Canadians perished by the score, Prime Minister Robert Borden moved reluctantly toward conscription. He perceived the situation as critical and called for the formation of a Union government.

Many Liberals accepted the call, but Laurier and French Canada refused to condone conscription. English-speaking press and churches cried for unity in the name of patriotism, and Laurier's party was driven back to its Quebec base in the election that followed on December 17, 1917.

The war years found King more and more alone.

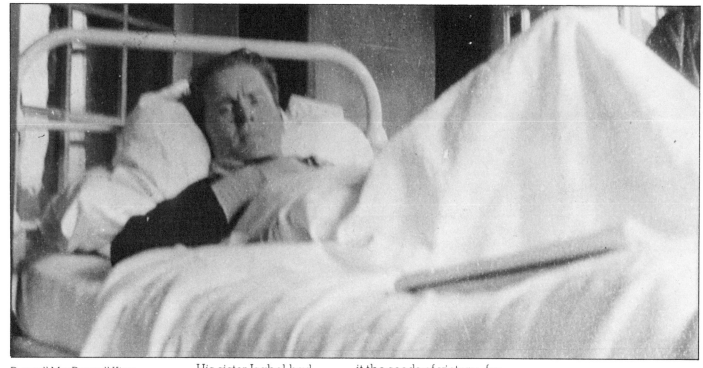

Dougall MacDougall King,
gravely ill

His sister Isabel had died in April, 1915; his father followed in August, 1916; his mother died in December, 1917; and his brother Dougall was terminally ill.

King's emotional isolation was matched only by his disappointment over his political defeat. But the defeat was to carry within it the seeds of victory, for he had lost at Laurier's side.

On February 17, 1919, the prime minister died.

King's reaction to the news was that "the Liberals of Quebec will never take as a leader any man who 'betrayed' Sir Wilfrid at the last election." He was right.

On August 7, 1919, William Lyon Mackenzie King was chosen federal Liberal party leader.

"Destiny has intended me to continue to carry on the fight which Grandfather commenced so bravely on behalf of the common people in their struggle," he confided in his diary.

THE WEATHER
Probabilities: Fair and cooler

PRICE TWO CENTS

The Globe.

TORONTO, FRIDAY, AUGUST 8, 1919—SIXTEEN PAGES.

The Net Circulation of The Globe During July, 1919, was 2,399,491, a Daily Average of **88,870**

VOL. LXXVI. NUMBER 21,706.

MACKENZIE KING ELECTED NEW LIBERAL LEADER

HON. MACKENZIE KING

MR. KING HAS MAJORITY ON THIRD BALLOT
HAVING 38 VOTES MORE THAN MR. FIELDING
QUEBEC ALMOST SOLIDLY FOR THE WINNER

As Liberal leader, King inherited the spoils of a strike that had recently traumatized Canada.

The Winnipeg General Strike had grown spontaneously from a series of strikes against the soaring cost of living. A substantial improvement was sought in wages and working conditions.

But Canadian industry, just coming into its own, demanded cooperation from its labour force.

Fears grew among businessmen and later governments and the Canadian public, that socialist elements were in control.

As The Royal North West Mounted Police and militia units filled the Winnipeg streets, other cities responded with sympathetic strikes. Indus-

trialists called for renewal of wartime censorship and other repressive legislation. Strike leaders were arrested, and strikers, understandably agitated, organized a march, intended to be peaceful, which was smashed on "Bloody Saturday" (June 21, 1919) by the Mounties. The Winnipeg Strike was

called off, but the country was left strongly divided.

A crowd overturns a Winnipeg streetcar during the strike

The Winnipeg Strike had symbolized all the hopes and frustrations of organized labour . . .

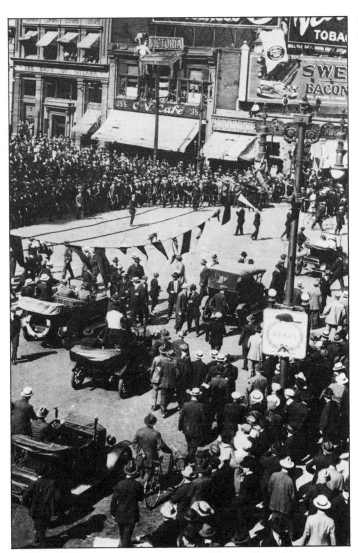

Labour and police confront each other in Winnipeg

...the bitter and unbending reaction of capital...

A torn Canada entered the second decade of the twentieth century, with French against English, rural against urban, east against west, and labour against capital.

The introduction of conscription had alienated Quebec Liberals, and King was faced with the difficult task of bringing anti-conscriptionist and conscriptionist Liberals back together to rebuild a truly national party. In July, 1920, Borden was replaced as prime minister by Arthur Meighen, the author of the 1917 conscription bill and symbol to French Canada of British imperialism.

and the cries of an unsympathetic public for conciliation and social stability.

English Canadians meanwhile agonized over liquor, and the puritan character of rural Ontario asserted itself by electing a United Farmer government. During the war years, Canadians had moved in great numbers from the austere farmhouses of rural communities to the bustle of the great cities. Tensions grew as the cities became increasingly insensitive to the rural interests. The farmers had begun to organize, calling for major tariff and freight-rate reductions, public ownership of utilities and natural resource development, and graduated taxes on private and corporate incomes and inherited estates. The platform was widely endorsed by rural political organizations. Federally, they supported the Progressive party.

Increasing wealth brought increasing problems.

Canadians were toying with affluence in the early 20's, and because wealth was so unevenly distributed, it proved a dangerous game. Tensions grew as the rich became increasingly intolerant of the poor. Large corporations seemed inhuman and dangerously powerful. Labour unions grew in size and strength and people began to talk about industrial cooperation and public ownership as means to restoring some semblance of social democracy. Strikes were numerous and violent.

Who could soothe these tensions?

Four men emerged as potential saviours.

Each promised a different road to the future.

Gaunt but forceful Arthur Meighen "was so logical," said the *Canadian Forum*, "that one could almost hear the clicking of his brain." Although eloquent and brilliant, Meighen was not a tactful politician. He was blunt, forthright and possessed a rigid sense of honour and integrity which, with his razor wit and caustic tongue, had won him enemies among French-Canadians and organized labour. He stood as a leader of the ruling class representing wealth and capital, thus supporting high tariffs. To Quebec, he also meant conscription.

Thomas Crerar, a Manitoba farmer, had been a Unionist Liberal and was Minister of Agriculture in 1917. He resigned in June of 1919, disgusted by the central-Canadian domination of the two major parties, and became leader of the Progressives. Crerar hoped that a large bloc of Progressives, "the true spirit of liberalism," could squeeze favourable legislation from the party in power. Although his sympathy was with the Liberals, he would make them work for his support.

James Shaver Woodsworth's integrity could not be doubted. The pacifist minister turned Christian Socialist was first elected as a Labour member of Parliament in 1921. His efforts on behalf of the Winnipeg strikers had resulted in his being jailed on a charge of sedition. For 21 years afterward, he would speak for society's weak and exploited with the zeal of a social visionary and the clarity of a prophet.

Mackenzie King rounded out the group. He reportedly said he would have liked to have been like Woodsworth if only it did not cost so much. King was as opaque as the other leaders were transparent – a referee, rather than a leader.

James Shaver Woodsworth; Mackenzie King; Arthur Meighen; Thomas Crerar

King refused to outline a clear policy during the 1921 election campaign. He wished to aggravate no one.

Campaigning in the West

On a western tour, he tried to bring the farmers back to the Liberal fold. King would let Meighen be hanged in Quebec by his imperialist stand, and would then present the Liberals as the only clearly national party.

"The man who can restore and foster a spirit of unity between city and country, between Ontario and Quebec on the one hand and Ontario and the West on the other hand, is the man of destiny."
The Canadian Forum, 1921

Mackenzie King eagerly produced both hands, and on December 29, 1921 the rebel's grandson took office as Prime Minister of Canada.

The 20's was a decade of progress and material utopia.

The "Spirit of St. Louis," which took Lindbergh across the Atlantic, was a symbol of technological progress

By 1923 Canada was experiencing economic prosperity. Export prices, particularly wheat, rose steadily while the price of manufactured goods fell. Pulp and paper mills, metal smelters and refineries, and transportation and communications industries flourished and expanded. Cars, tele- phones, and abundant electricity symbolized prosperity.

Flappers, séances,
fortune-telling and auto
touring – all were
fashionable.

Fortune-telling at a Toronto estate

Motion pictures boomed, and fads flourished.

Douglas Fairbanks and Canada's Mary Pickford, box-office stars of the 20's

The 20's also witnessed a renaissance in Canadian art.

Poets and artists stopped imitating Europeans and began to discover their Canadian identity.

"The Solemn Land" by J.E.H. MacDonald

It was also a decade of a growing population...

With prosperity and a new wheat boom, thousands of hopeful immigrants crowded Canadian docks. The dream of the New World often died, however, in the nightmare of immigrant sheds in Winnipeg, where new Canadians gathered to purchase farmland. The less fortunate and those without capital ended up in city slums or victimized by industry.

But for many a new life in Canada meant independence, freedom and prosperity. In return, immigrants developed the nation and contributed their own culture to the national identity.

...and growing nationalism.

In 1927 Canada celebrated her sixtieth anniversary. The jubilee celebrations held in July gave Canadians a chance to revel in the strong sense of identity being expressed in all areas of Canadian culture.

A scene on Parliament Hill

The first world war had given Canada a new independent status in international relations.

At the League of Nations
in Geneva, her delegates
signed her own treaties.

Britain, on the other hand, sought stronger imperial unity in foreign affairs.

King saw a danger for Canada in diplomatic unity – once again, the country could be involved in an imperial war.

He cautiously asserted Canadian autonomy in foreign affairs, and was jubilant when the Imperial Conference in London in 1926 defined the Dominions as "autonomous communities within the British Empire, equal in status, in no way subordinate one to another in any aspect of their domestic or external affairs, though united by a common allegiance to the Crown and freely associated as members of the British Commonwealth of Nations."

Delegates to the Imperial Conference of 1923

King reflected the hopes of the Canadian public. The casualties, fatherless homes and national divisions caused by the first world war were well remembered, and many Canadians, secure and comfortable in the prosperity of the 20's, preferred to turn inward, away from European diplomacy.

King's leadership assumed a low profile – but he was far from idle.

The prime minister and his cabinet appeared to Canadians as faceless, austere administrators, unwilling to rock the boat. But King's energies were being spent in mending his divided party and nation.

King took office in 1921 with a narrow majority government. He was determined to bring the country together, to conciliate, and carefully follow public opinion. There were sixty farmer M.P.'s in the House – he could smell the political manure.

While creating the impression of "business as usual" to high-tariff Toronto and Montreal manufacturers, he attempted to lure the Progressives back to the Liberal party with promises of progressive legislation and lower tariffs. In truth, King played upon the differences among the Progressive members, and, beginning with T.A. Crerar, absorbed them slowly into the government.

Meanwhile, King managed with remarkable diplomacy to avoid being identified with either faction. His foreign policy – one of no commitments – was acceptable to the majority of Canadians and offensive to almost no one. In a bland, lifeless way he was providing the leadership he felt was necessary in Canada in the 1920's.

King went to the people in October, 1925, satisfied that his invisible government was all the voters wanted.

The voters, however, were not as confident of King. They elected 116 Conservatives, 99 Liberals, 24 Progressives, and 6 Independent members. King's future might well have been one of obscurity, but he cleverly managed to recover his parliamentary majority, defeat the Conservatives, and banish his arch-rival Arthur Meighen as leader of the Conservative party.

His prize – the first minority government in Canadian history.

King advised Governor General Lord Byng of Vimy, that he would carry on with Progressive support until defeated in the House of Commons. Lord Byng believed that King, with no seat in Parliament, should resign, and Arthur Meighen, whose Conservative party held the largest number of seats in the House of Commons, should form a government. King insisted on Parliament's right to decide if his government could continue, and the Liberals, with their leader sitting in the gallery, faced the House.

Every vote was crucial. The insecure government went to work at once to win Progressive and Labour support.

King moved cautiously and prudently, saying little. Tax reductions passed easily. Under pressure from Labour members J.S. Woodsworth and A.A. Heaps, a bill authorizing old age pensions passed. King willingly placated the independent members of the left, hoping to show up the Conservatives as reactionary in contrast.

Then, the storm broke. A special committee investigating the Customs and Excise Department revealed gross scandals connecting civil servants with smuggling. The Progressives seemed likely to withdraw their support and bring down the government.

King suddenly changed his mind about letting Parliament decide. He could not allow the Progressives to censure his government in the House of Commons, and asked Governor General Lord Byng for dissolution. It was an unusual request since King, in theory, had no reason for dissolution. Byng, a forthright and high-minded ex-soldier, refused to dissolve Parliament.

King was astonished. He felt it was the duty of the governor-general to accept the prime minister's advice. Byng, on the other hand, believed it was his duty to keep King to his word and have Parliament decide.

THE VAMP

1914 – WILLIE KING, FRIEND OF LABOR – 1917

HON. W. L. M. KING—"I have done everything to vamp labor except get my hair bobbed; that will be the next thing."

King resigned and Meighen took office. After just three days, Meighen's government was defeated in the House by a single vote. Lord Byng granted Meighen dissolution, and voters were asked to go to the polls in September, 1926, for the second time within a year.

Whatever other results Lord Byng's action may have had, it is certain that in refusing to be guided by Mr. King's advice he saved the bacon of the Liberal party."

The Canadian Forum

King poured his feelings of relief into his diary. "I could not believe Byng would deliver himself so completely into my hands or [to] give Meighen a dissolution on top of a defeat sustained within 2½ days of his taking office... Like Saul I need to see the light. The light has come, has come around me in this crisis. 'The God of our fathers hath chosen me' – as he did Saul...I see it all so clearly. From now on, I go forward in the strength of God and His Might and Right to battle as my forefathers battled for the rights of the people – and God's will on earth 'even as it is done in Heaven'."

In this mood of almost hysterical elation King entered the political battlefield. His mission had never seemed so clear: he would fight for responsible government – for political liberty against autocratic British rule, as his grandfather had done. He recorded in his diary that his mother's God was with him during the campaign. The public could not have failed to be impressed by his conviction.

In fact there was something other than "God's Will" involved in the 1926 election. Meighen and his party were like the bright shades of summer clothing – colourful, but not something Canadians wanted to wear all the time. They preferred more neutral hues, and who was more neutral than bland, plodding Mackenzie King? He could be likened to a serviceable grey suit that might be worn to either a wedding or a funeral.

King won a majority government and Arthur Meighen, defeated and bitter, resigned as Conservative leader. He was replaced by Richard Bedford Bennett, a millionaire lawyer from Calgary.

Mackenzie King was in his fifties during the late 1920's and still a bachelor. Physically he was an unimpressive man. "I do not like my appearance anywhere – a little fat round man, no expression of a lofty character," he wrote.

He had other qualities as a leader, however. He was flexible, conciliatory, pragmatic, quick to spot and use talent or weaknesses in others, always keenly aware of public opinion, and not offensive to Quebeckers.

The frustrated, overdriven Willie King had become an astute manipulator. He had learned how to control and influence people without commanding them. Problems were couched in moralistic and vague language, and he was even guilty of prevarication. But he managed to project himself to Canadians as their chief conciliator. In later years in office he would be presented as the only alternative to chaos.

He lived alone, but he was not alone.

"Matters of friendship," he wrote, "cannot be accompanied by too much in the way of reserve."

King had few, if any, close friends. Instead he poured his loneliness onto the thousands of pages of the diary he kept for 57 years.

With the death of his brother Dougall in 1922, only his sister Jennie remained of his once close family. Jennie now had a family and concerns of her own.

King could not accept the deaths of the other family members and continued to believe they guided him from beyond

the grave. "I believe dear mother and father and Max and Bell are near and about me and Sir Wilfrid as well. Their spirits will guide and protect me," he wrote. In this way he did not feel alone, for the spirits played the dual role of guiding him on his foreordained path and buffering him from his pro-

found isolation.

The dead insulated him from the living.

He divided his days between Laurier House and Kingsmere.

In 1921, upon Lady Laurier's death, King had inherited Laurier House in Ottawa. A number of wealthy Liberals renovated and furnished the house for King, and he resided there for the rest of his life.

The only exception was the days he spent, especially in summer, at Kingsmere, his country estate twelve miles outside of Ottawa. Kingsmere was his refuge, and a symbol of his isolation.

Laurier House, Ottawa

King and his sister Jennie

King, a friend and O.D. Skelton, under-secretary in the Department of External Affairs, at Kingsmere

At Kingsmere, he could play the role of "country gentleman."

From his roomy farmhouse perched on a hillside, he could overlook his woods, stream, lake and the field where his sheep grazed. The experiment with sheep proved a failure, however, and after dogs and disease diminished their numbers, he gave them up.

He later collected ruins of historic buildings, beginning with the remnants of an Ottawa home that had belonged to Simon-Napoleon Parent, once premier of Quebec. The ruins included stones that had been replaced at the British House of Parliament, stones from the Canadian Parliament buildings, and pieces of various Ottawa landmarks.

King referred to his collection as "the cloisters" or "the temple," and he relaxed by walking alone among them. Although he affected the role of squire, he was more like a spinster fussing over his infertile estate.

King was attracted to women and spent considerable time in their company.

But he never met one with all the qualities he sought in a wife.

King and lady friends at Kingsmere

King and his dogs

King had three Irish terriers between 1924 and his death; all were called "Pat."

Each slept in a little basket at the foot of his master's bed, ate with him, greeted him in the evenings, and listened intently for news from Parliament Hill. King enjoyed this rather empty domestic life. After a guest left Laurier House, he wrote that he felt a "real sense of rest and freedom in being...alone with Pat at breakfast and no need to be thinking of engagements of others."

In his isolation, King found himself moving slowly toward spiritualism.

Though quick to adjust to the new problems of 20th century society, King had always been drawn to the unseen world. As early as 1896 he had dabbled with fortunetellers. He was certain that men and society moved in ways other than material, and that the spiritual universe could and did inspire the material. All that King had deeply loved was dead: mother, father, Mac, Bella, Sir Wilfrid, and the Victorian ideals that he worshipped. He had to have reassurance and direction, and, for King, it must come from the most spiritually pure source.

In life, and after her death, he had idealized the motivation received from his mother. He could not be without her. His father, Laurier and others were also important. Surely they would not leave him?

He saw the spiritual light first in small cracks, such as coincidences. If he was troubled about some thought or action and noticed that the hands of the clock were in a straight line, he was relieved and felt that "some presence" was letting him know that he was "on the right line." Dreams and chance meetings served to emphasize the closeness of the spiritual world, and the spirits' direction of his life seemed always apparent.

But survival on the earthly plane took priority with the crash of North America's stock markets in 1929.

The age of paper profits and confidence in unlimited business expansion ground to a halt with the crash of the New York, Toronto and Montreal stock exchanges. The world paused for a moment of anxious silence. But no one guessed in 1929 the seriousness of the economic collapse.

King did not understand the Depression.

UNTO CAESAR

TORY
PROVINCE
UNEMPLOYED

No one cent from
Federal Treasury to
Tory Provincial
Tory Government
for Unemployment
Purposes

WILLIAM REX

HON. W. L. M. KING—"Aside, knave, I give only those who worship Caesar." Tel. April 7, '93.

He did not believe prosperity was at an end, but thought the economy and unemployment were undergoing a natural, temporary downturn. As provincial governments failed to meet relief costs, King was criticized for not coming to their rescue. He declared in the House that he would not subsidize any Tory provincial government. To those truculent Tory governments who had opposed his government, he "would not give them a five cent piece."

His misunderstanding of the gravity of the economic situation and his clearly partisan approach were resented by voters. In July, 1930, they elected a Conservative government.

The Crash meant deprivation...

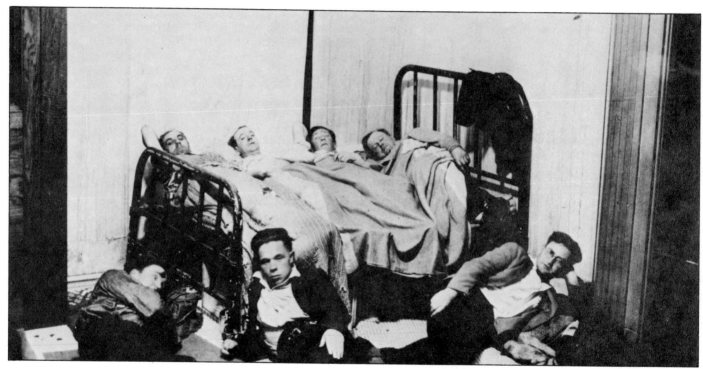

Stock prices fell, companies closed their doors, unemployment rose and consumer spending fell. A drought in the West had reduced drastically the amount of wheat for export, which meant that the railways – Canada's largest employer – were forced to cut back.

By 1933 nearly a million Canadians were unemployed, out of a population of approximately ten million.

despair . . .

"What can these people do? They have been driven from our parks; they have been driven from our streets; they have been driven from our buildings, and in this city they actually took refuge on the garbage heaps."
J.S. Woodsworth

At the darkest hour of the Depression about two million Canadians, or one out of five, were dependent on some form of state aid. Yet relief was given grudgingly, and to only the absolutely destitute. Even then relief payments were barely enough to subsist. Worse, a recipient could be cut off if his neighbour reported that he owned a radio.

One disheartened Winnipeg father who had been many months on relief wrote directly to Prime Minister R.B. Bennett in June, 1933: "You stated that there would be no one starve in Canada. I presume you meant not starve over night but slowly our family amongst thousands of others are doing the same slowly and slowly.

Possibly you have never felt the Pang of a Wolf. Well become a Father have children then have them come to you asking for a slice of bread between meals and have to tell them to wait. Wait until five of humanitys humans sleep all in one room no larger than nine square feet with one window in it...For God's sake please make a personal endeavour to assist me toward a brighter outlook immediately."

The prime minister received thousands such letters.

122

relief camps . . .

In 1932, the federal government began to finance work camps for single homeless men under the auspices of the Department of National Defence. The men worked for their clothing, room and board, and received 20 cents a day.

For many, relief was a nightmare of humiliation by fatuous bureaucrats. The work they were made to do at relief camps nearly always provided nothing of value, and their self esteem tumbled while their frustration grew.

...and radical politics.

In early summer, 1935, an army of hungry and frustrated young men began a march on Ottawa from Kamloops, B.C. They were joined by hundreds of other angry young men on their way east.

On Dominion Day, they stopped at Regina for an open-air rally to plan their demonstration. They were met by Dominion and local police who, in attempting to break up the peaceful meeting, killed one man and injured countless others.

The government, although sympathetic to property owners, seemed ill-prepared to heed the psychological and material plight of the dispossessed. Nor could they.

Richard Bedford Bennett, the millionaire lawyer-businessman who lived in a suite of 17 rooms at Ottawa's Chateau Laurier Hotel, led his Conservative government through the worst of the "dirty thirties."

Bennett was not an insensitive man, but like Mackenzie King, he could not understand the Depression. He promised immediate action and provided $20 million to the provinces for relief work. But he had no overall plan. Bennett raised the tariff and saved many Canadian firms from bankruptcy, but in so doing kept the price of imported goods unnecessarily high, compounding the plight of those living at subsistence level.

The tariff failed to stimulate enough production to relieve the country's massive unemployment problem.

Bennett was handicap-

ped by two factors: an orthodox economic doctrine and the public's misinformed attitude that the business community alone could recover the lost days of prosperity.

No one really knew how to deal with industrial depression.

Nothing Bennett tried worked. The economist, John Maynard Keynes, and his followers called for massive government spending to stimulate the economy, but Bennett, like King, felt this was economic heresy. Orthodox economics called for retrenchment in hard times; thus, retrenchment and relief were prescribed.

Bennett reflected the perplexity prevalent among economists and businessmen when in 1931 he wrote: "The difficulty about all these matters is that too much reliance is being placed upon the Government. The people are not bearing their share of the load.

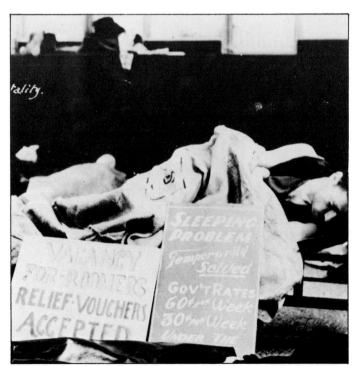

Half a century ago people would work their way out of their difficulties rather than look to a government to take care of them . . . I do not know what the result of the present movement may be, but unless it induces men and women to think in terms of honest toil rather than in terms of bewilderment because of conditions which they helped to create, the end of organized society is not far distant."

"We are the growing generation of Canadians, but with no hope of a future."

A young, single man wrote to the prime minister, trying to explain his plight: "Now I am wandering the streets like a beggar, with no future ahead...There are plenty of young men like myself, who are in the same plight. I say again what is to be done for us single men? do we have to starve? or do we have to go round with our faces full of shame, to beg at the doors of the well to do citizen...Did you ever feel the pangs of hunger? My idea is we shall all starve."

Some had a simple solution for the prime minister.

"We have decided
that in a month from this date,
if thing's are the same,
we'll skin you alive,
the first chance we get."
  The Sudbury Starving Unemployed

Others had a grander vision.

J.S. Woodsworth addressing
workers and the unemployed

Perhaps no one questioned the economic and social order more articulately than J.S. Woodsworth. In 1933 alone he made over 200 political addresses, from Victoria to Sydney, seeking "change by bloodless means."

A coalition of labour, Marxists, farmers and socialists called themselves the "Cooperative Commonwealth Federation." They sought a new social order that would replace capitalism with a socialist-democratic state.

Meanwhile, King was seeking reassurance from those he wanted near him.

In 1932 he attended a séance at which the medium was the famous Mrs. Etta Wriedt. Through Mrs. Wriedt, he finally believed he had achieved direct communications with his mother. He also "spoke" to Sir Wilfrid Laurier, Bert Harper, grandfather Mackenzie and the other family members. King was thrilled, and invited Mrs. Wriedt to Ottawa where other séances were undertaken.

When Canadians went to the polls on October 14, 1935, to decide between re-electing Bennett's Conservative government or electing a new one, King already knew the results. They had been forecast to him the evening before from the spirit world. Sir Wilfrid Laurier had predicted a decisive victory for the Liberals. And the spirit of Lord Grey, a former governor-general, told him: "Long ago I saw that you would be a peace-maker ...God has chosen you for that purpose."

In 1934 King felt a resurgence of energy and confidence. Jolted from his sleep by a "vision," he realized "it is mother who has been bringing all this about as an angel of God ...I had a very clear vision of some man who seemed to be possessed of great power, and of its being exerted upon a woman in a manner which seemed to leave her without vitality, and as it were 'dematerialized', in her stead there seemed to be layer upon layer of illustrated pictures, many of them sensual in character ...He left her to materialize as it were, and himself mounted a horse like a Prussian."

The experience seemed to reassure King, on the verge of political ascension, of his sense of mission, and he continued his crusade through politics. His lady in the other world had given him the power.

Lord Grey

133

Sir Wilfrid was right.

The Liberal slogan for the 1935 election was "King or Chaos," reflecting the nation's concern over Bennett's radical proposals. King, as always, seemed a safe choice. Canadians re-elected King's Liberals with a vengeance.

Back in office, King's style of government continued unchanged. In external affairs King followed the policies of his mentor, Sir Wilfrid. He made no commitments to collective security arrangements within the British Commonwealth. He still remembered the conflict caused by the conscription question and its effect on the nation and, above all, on his Liberal party.

On a deeper level, King, like most Canadians in the 1930's, sincerely wanted to avoid involvement in the intricacies of European diplomacy, with its possible extension — war.

Meanwhile, events in the Rhineland were bringing world history to a turning point.

German troops entering the Rhineland

The treaty of Versailles, which settled the first world war, provided that Germany's industrial Rhineland would continue to be a demilitarized zone after allied military occupation had ended. Having already violated the treaty by introducing rearmament and conscription, Hitler proceeded to re-occupy the Rhineland's great industrial armaments centres, posing an even greater threat to the French frontier.

The Nazis might have been stopped at this point, but appeasers and isolationists – especially in Britain – were anxious to avoid military confrontation. Overwhelming public sentiment in the western world favoured peace, and British diplomats refused to go to war with Germany "for walking into their own backyard."

King, who did not want Canada dragged into a European conflict, was silent. In private, he encouraged the British government to appease Hitler.

Franklin Roosevelt, seen by many Americans as the great friend of the people, was greatly admired in Canada.

The American president and Mackenzie King became fast friends during the 30's. The friendship proved to be important for furthering Anglo-American cooperation in years to come.

On domestic economic policy, however, the two leaders differed. King was far more cautious than Roosevelt, and had not yet been converted to the policy of massive government spending to stimulate a depressed economy.

At Roosevelt's invitation King travelled to Washington in March, 1937, to discuss trade agreements and the proposed Canadian-

American St. Lawrence Seaway Development project.

The American government also had hopes of negotiating a trade agreement with Great Britain, and Roosevelt wanted King to use his influence in London on America's behalf. King and Roosevelt talked for

several hours, with King encouraging closer American-British ties.

King favoured the creation of a permanent international organization where world social and economic problems could be discussed. He sincerely wanted to promote peace, and was encouraged by Roosevelt's support.

King was now ready to move on to Britain for the Imperial Conference where he would present, as he told Roosevelt, "a North American background."

137

1937 was the 100th anniversary of William Lyon Mackenzie's rebellion.

King felt confident on his arrival in London in May for the Imperial Conference. Britain wanted the Dominions to endorse British commitments to Belgium and France, but King fought cooperation among Commonwealth members on the grounds that it encroached on Canadian sovereignty over her own external affairs.

Pleased with himself, he wrote," It was a singular thing that at the end of 100 years, I was contending in No. 10 Downing Street, for a policy that would preserve the Empire while preserving national freedom to its parts, the very thing my grandfather was fighting for a hundred years ago."

King with His Majesty King George VI at the Imperial Conference in London, 1937

King had a "vision" of his role in world affairs.

Mackenzie King at the All-German Sports Competition, Berlin, 1937

In his vision, he saw himself furthering the cause of world peace.

He travelled to Germany to see firsthand Hitler's Third Reich, and while there, told the Fuehrer that they had much in common. He explained that in his hometown, Berlin, Ontario, there were many of German descent. He also warned Hitler that Canada would support Britain if she were attacked. But King was "deeply impressed with the great constructive work" Hitler had achieved in Germany.

Like many other politicians, King failed to understand the full meaning of the rise of Nazi Germany.

In March, 1938, Germany annexed Austria. Soon after, Nazi Germans in Sudetenland, Czechoslovakia, began to clamour for annexation of the Sudetenland to the Fatherland. By August, Hitler was threatening to invade Czechoslovakia, and the world faced a seemingly inevitable war.

Mackenzie King felt he was perched at the very edge of political oblivion. If war came, Canada would again be divided and the Liberal party shattered. All that he had worked for – national unity, the political dominance of the Liberal party, world peace, and greater cooperation among the English-speaking nations – might be lost. All during September, as the European powers negotiated, he agonized. Should he announce Canada's support of Britain in case of a European war and risk alienating his French cabinet ministers?

Some Canadians demanded that Canada support Britain unequivocally. Many Liberals, North American nationalists, and French-Canadians, however, demanded that Canada pursue an isolationist course. King decided to wait until war had been declared.

Toward the end of September he felt more hopeful. Hitler, France's Daladier, England's Chamberlain and Italy's Mussolini met at Munich, and Chamberlain returned with a declaration of peace. The Munich agreement allowed Germany to occupy the Sudetenland in exchange for Hitler's promise to halt further eastward expansion.

Mackenze King was overjoyed at the prospect of peace.

King decided to write to Hitler.

In February, 1939, King reminded Hitler that Canada would stand behind Great Britain. Indeed, Canadian defence expenditures were being sharply increased. A concerned King warned Hitler that war would destroy everything that he (Hitler) had accomplished for Germany.

"You will, I know accept this letter in the spirit in which it was written — an expression of the faith I have in the purpose you have at heart, and of the friendship with yourself which you have been so kind as to permit me to share."

143

Nazi expansion continued.

Canadian military status was still a mystery to Canadians and to foreign states when, in March, 1939, Hitler's armies seized Prague and Czechoslovakia fell under Nazi rule.

British Prime Minister Chamberlain announced that a German invasion of Poland would mean war.

On September 1, 1939, German artillery screamed across the Polish countryside.

The skies grew dark with Nazi aircraft, and Hitler's invading armies betrayed the real aims behind Nazi diplomacy — mastery of all Europe.

Two days later, Britain and France were at war with Germany.

Prime Minister King immediately announced that Canada's Parliament would be summoned to declare war and fight at Britain's side.

How deeply, Canadians wondered, would they become involved?

King could not forget what conscription had done to the Liberal party in 1917. Now his mission was to keep Canada united in its war effort. King decided to tread cautiously.

The first challenge to King's war policy came from Premier Maurice Duplessis of Quebec.

Ernest Lapointe and Maurice Duplessis

Duplessis' small conservative following in the Quebec legislature had joined with dissident Liberals in 1936 to form the Union Nationale. Duplessis contended that involvement in the European war would destroy Quebec's provincial autonomy. He called a provincial election for the fall of 1939, seeking an emergency mandate with which to fight Ottawa's encroachment on Quebec's provincial rights.

In response, Ernest Lapointe, Minister of Justice and King's oldest and closest associate, toured Quebec preaching the virtue of the federal government's military policy. He also assured his fellow Quebeckers that he would resign along with other Quebec ministers if Duplessis were re-elected. French Canada would then face an imposed conscription by a government dominated by English-Canadians. It was the biggest gamble of

Lapointe's career, and it succeeded. Duplessis was defeated and Quebec voted in a Liberal government under Adelard Godbout.

For the duration of the war King walked a tightrope between Quebec's isolationism and English Canada's demand for increased military involvement.

Gunnery practice at RCAF gunnery school in Jarvis, Ontario

Fortunately for King, the war in Europe moved slowly during the first six months, and any kind of increased Canadian commitment could be regarded as over-reactionary.

A safe way of making a commitment appeared in late September, 1939. British Prime Minister Chamberlain was faced with a desperate need to expand the British air force. He required 50,000 air crew annually, and since Britain did not have the resources to produce the training facilities, he proposed establishing training schools in Canada, Australia, and New Zealand, with advanced training to take place in Canada. Graduating airmen would be at the disposal of the British government.

On December 17, King signed the British Commonwealth Air Training Agreement. He was delighted. The scheme enabled Canada to contribute without further direct involvement in the war. Canada had already sent the first Canadian Division, approximately 20,000 men, to England for training. This was a safe, cautious, moderate move.

But some dissenting voices would not be stilled.

Ontario Premier Mitchell Hepburn was an honest, forthright democrat and reformer, but he was also quarrelsome, vindictive and prone to political grandstanding. He continually reminded the Ontario public that although he was a Liberal, he was not a "Mackenzie King Liberal," and he told them in 1938 that "Mackenzie King never did like Ontario."

King was publicly cool to Hepburn, but privately detested him.

When he learned that Hepburn had contracted bronchial pneumonia in the summer of 1940, he confided in his diary: "If this is so, it probably means the end of his earthly life. I don't often wish that a man should pass away, but I believe it would be the most fortunate thing that could happen at this time." Ironically, Hepburn, in seeking to destroy King, forced him to make one of the most fortunate decisions of his political career.

On January 18, 1940, King was bitterly denounced in the Ontario legislature by Conservative leader Colonel George Drew. Drew felt that King and his federal Liberals were providing insufficient support to Great Britain. Premier Hepburn agreed, and calmly asked to be associated with Colonel Drew in censuring the King government.

Provincial Liberals were scandalized.

King welcomed a confrontation with Hepburn, for he was sure of support from the Canadian people.

On January 15, 1940, while in his study preparing for that afternoon's opening of the new session of Parliament, he was seized with an idea of how to rid himself of the troublesome Hepburn and win the federal election at the same time. He would dissolve Parliament that very day and call an election on the issue of Canada's war effort.

In the spring of 1940, King was 65 years old, with almost 15 years' experience as prime minister. By now he was an astute politician, and had correctly guessed the mood of the public. In the temperate climate of "the phony war," federal Conservative leader Manion's demand for a Union government seemed extreme and ill-considered.

King's government was given resounding support; 181 Liberals were returned, compared to 40 Conservatives, and only 8 C.C.F. members.

King's victory came just in time.

In late spring of 1940, Hitler's war machine moved into high gear. Denmark, Norway, Holland, Belgium, Luxembourg and France fell into the grip of the Gestapo.

The fall of France in June, 1940, changed the war for Canada. Many Canadians, shocked by the realization that now Britain was vulnerable, began to call for an expanded war effort. The Opposition called for the prime minister's resignation.

In a compromise measure, the National Resources Mobilization Act, giving the government broad powers to mobilize all the nation's resources, including conscription for home defence, was quickly passed. Voluntary service increased dramatically, and on Christmas Day, 1940, the Canadian Corps was formed under General A.G.L. McNaughton.

Canadian industry boomed and unemployment fell to zero as the economy moved to full production to meet war needs.

The country plunged in, with mounting participation and sacrifices for the war effort.

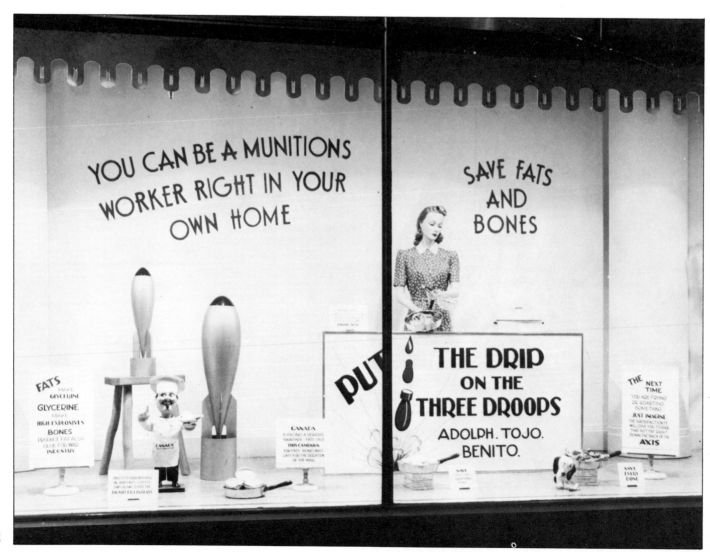

King had formed a warm relationship with President Roosevelt.

In August, 1940, King had met Roosevelt at Ogdensburg, New York, where the two leaders agreed to create a Permanent Joint Board on Defence.

The Permanent Joint Board on Defence met in Ottawa later that month. Both the U.S. and Canada were represented equally, and the Board served to ensure that Canadian interests would be recognized in the defence of North America.

An economic agreement in April, 1941, paved the way for closer cooperation between Canada and the U.S. The Hyde Park Declaration, which followed a meeting between King and Roosevelt at Hyde Park, ensured that Canada and the U.S. would provide each other with the defence materials that each could produce most capably.

As a result, Americans would buy more Canadian goods and the large Canadian deficit in favour of the U.S. would be brought into balance.

Between 1939 and 1942 Canada would experience a social and economic transformation.

To meet Britain's pressing demands for goods, Canadian shipyards would build corvettes, frigates and mine-sweepers, and Canadian industry would produce small arms, light trainers for the Air Training Plan, Hurricane fighters, Hampden bombers and munitions.

Before the end of 1942, England would purchase over three billion dollars' worth of war materials from Canada. That same year, King's government would subsidize a billion dollars' worth of British purchases, thus helping war-ravaged Britain and continuing the flow of Canada's wartime prosperity.

During the war King increasingly relied on the advice of his experts.

King's government was dominated by Clarence Decatur Howe, an ambitious and enterprising businessman-turned-politician who was given the task of "defence procurement and industrial mobilization." He was quickly dubbed "Minister of Everything" for the singlehanded way he engineered domestic war operations, although officially he was minister of transport.

King relied heavily on Howe's talent and duties as he did his other ministers. But he chose not to form close personal friendships with his colleagues, preferring to keep the relationships "professional."

King worked alone at Laurier House, running his secretarial staff ragged.

C.D. Howe, King's "Minister of Everything" was largely responsible for organizing Canada's war effort.

Ernest Lapointe was his closest advisor and Quebec lieutenant until his death in 1941, when Louis St. Laurent became King's strongest Quebec minister.

C.G. Power, his minister of national defence for air, devised a plan whereby a number of cabinet committees would supervise various war operations. Most important of these was the War Committee of Cabinet, consisting of the prime minister, the minister of finance, the minister of national defence and other senior cabinet ministers.

Despite the efficient operation of King's government and his ministers' high profiles, Mackenzie King remained in the shadow of Winston Churchill, Britain's new prime minister.

But his pale image as a war leader began to cause him concern.

His speech during Canada's declaration of war sounded more like a lawyer's brief than a call to arms. He knew that his grey, uninspiring public image could obscure his divinely inspired mission: the successful emergence through the war, of a united Canada, with closer British-American ties. He worried that Churchill's forthright qualities as a war leader would outshine his own subtle ones.

King reproached himself for not having devoted more time to rhetoric and public speaking, and was disappointed with his national broadcasts. He hired a famous speech writer to assist him in the future, and asked John Grierson, the talented government film commissioner, to help him improve his public image. He determined, whenever possible, to be more visible to the Canadian public.

But at least one group of Canadians did not buy his "new image."

In August, 1941, King travelled to Britain and visited the Canadian armed forces. He confided to his diary that he "would have given anything not to have to speak [to the troops]," but General McNaughton strongly advised it.

"From one part of the grandstand to the right there was considerable booing as I was leaving the stand to go across to inspect the Guard [of Honour]."

King inspecting the guard of honour

King felt certain the booing had been organized by the "Tories," but when he spoke again later more booing was heard. Canadian newspapers gave the incident considerable coverage, and King's image suffered as a result.

The booing, however, proved to be an isolated incident, and despite King's terror at speaking to the troops, he was thereafter well received.

General McNaughton observes as King addresses his troops

In December, 1941, Churchill arrived in Canada for an official visit.

While in England, King had opposed Canadian participation in an Imperial War Cabinet, partly because he knew it would be dominated by Churchill. King mistrusted Churchill; indeed, before the war he considered him a dangerous warmonger. But Churchill was a brilliant and successful leader — the right man for the times — and King's opinion began to change after the Battle of Britain.

When Churchill visited Ottawa, King demanded and received assurance that the British-American pledge to give full resources to the war effort would not pressure Canada into accepting conscription.

Churchill addressed both houses of Parliament.

"Let us then address ourselves to our task,
not in any way underrating its tremendous difficulties and
perils, but in good heart and sober confidence, resolve
that whatever the cost, whatever the suffering,
we shall stand by each other,
true and faithful comrades,
to do our duty, God helping us,
to the end."

Churchill listened patiently to King's description of Canada's complex politics, but he seemed puzzled by King's methods of governing.

"Why don't you assert your authority, say that you want it and have it done," he advised.

But King played his politics to a more subtle tune.

"I shall fight on with a view of the war being won without resort to conscription," he wrote in his diary." Certainly my vision, I think, is clearer."

On December, 7, 1941, a storm of Japanese bombs rained down on the American fleet at Pearl Harbor. The United States had entered the war.

Japanese-Canadians in British Columbia were immediately interned in camps.

"Not necessarily conscription, but conscription if necessary."
Mackenzie King, 1942

After Pearl Harbor the United States government introduced compulsory military service, and Canadian newspapers — especially in Toronto — began vigorously agitating for conscription in Canada. King refused to renege on his commitment to fight the war without conscription, even though his minister of defence, J.L. Ralston, was asking for a larger army.

Hoping to stall for time, King proposed a plebiscite. The government, in this way, sought freedom to impose conscription "if it became necessary," as King averred in his famous phrase.

The controversial phrase provoked a new crisis in French Canada.

In November, 1941, Arthur Meighen was again chosen leader of the national Conservative party. He stood clearly for the policy of immediate conscription and total war effort. His leadership, followed by King's proposed plebiscite, convinced the French-Canadians that they were being railroaded into accepting conscription.

Georges Pelletier, André Laurendeau and others founded La Ligue pour la Defense du Canada. They sponsored meetings and advertisements and toured Quebec promoting a "no" to King's request for release from his pledge not to impose

conscription for overseas service. They did not object to conscription for service in Canada, but they would never accept compulsory service for war in other parts of the world.

The vote on the plebiscite took place on April 27, 1942. Quebec solidly opposed releasing the prime minister from his pledge;

English Canada voted for "conscription if necessary." P.J.A. Cardin resigned from King's ministry over the plebiscite results, leaving Louis St. Laurent the only Quebec minister.

King's mission — to preserve the unity of Canada — was, like the ship of state, perched precariously on the rocks. A sud-

den change in the winds of fate might ground his government and destroy his mission.

Henri Bourassa, influential French-Canadian nationalist and lifelong opponent of conscription, joined with the Ligue pour la Defense du Canada in denouncing conscription and advocated a resounding "no" in the plebiscite.

King and his defence minister clashed on the need for conscription.

King's solution was to remove the clause in the National Resources Mobilization Act that permitted conscripts to serve only in Canada. He did not, however, impose conscription, and insisted he would not until it was "necessary."

J.L. Ralston, King's defence minister, felt conscription for overseas service was necessary and urgent. He interpreted the results of the plebiscite to mean that the country supported the government in imposing conscription.

When King countered that Parliament would decide when conscription was necessary and not the

minister of defence, Ralston tendered his resignation. King did not accept it and Ralston carried on, although it was clear that King was working with a divided cabinet. For now he would take no action. As he reminded Ralston, he was "a great believer in events determining situations."

Dieppe.

By summer, 1942, the British were not ready for a major assault on Nazi Europe, but decided that raids would provide valuable experience and information for a future invasion. Dieppe, once a fashionable French summer resort, was a port of major significance, and it was decided that here a direct attack, sheltered by British naval firepower, should be made.

On August 19, 1942, the Second Canadian Division met with slaughter as the first rays of sunlight refracted across the English Channel. British and American press sang the glories of their respective efforts, but the cold, brutal facts were that the raid was a disaster. Canadians paid for it with over 2700 killed or captured.

The Canadian sacrifice at Dieppe was a bitter lesson.

Canadians obviously needed representation on the British-American boards and agencies of war operations. King wanted Canadian views recognized particularly where her interests were at stake.

Canada's position between the two giants was bound up with King's own image. Even in Canada, Churchill and Roosevelt were thought of as "our leaders." King's pale image had cast him among the shadows where he blended in so well.

Churchill, Roosevelt and King at the Pacific War Council, 1943

"The grey and the white" faced French-Canadians at the Quebec Conference of 1943.

On August 23, Churchill and Mackenzie King drove together through the streets of Quebec. King recorded in his diary: "Indeed as we looked at the people from the car, it was like a vast throng hailing a deliverer. Churchill was dressed in a white linen suit. At times, he sat up at the back of the car. I had a grey suit and was careful to remain seated except for a moment at the City Hall."

King said of Field Marshal Montgomery: "He has a manner of a mystic who sees into the future quite clearly . . . and is sustained by a vision which is beyond the immediate perils and dangers."

By the summer of 1944, the Allies were ready for their full-scale invasion of Europe. The assault would come in three waves: from Italy northward, from Russia westward, and from our Allied landing in Western Europe. King's hope was to have Canadian participation "on a token basis with forces that are wholly and exclusively Canadian, fighting as such but under American command."

But Canadian involvement was more than token.

Field Marshal Sir Bernard Montgomery visits General H.D.G. Crerar in Holland

The Canadian army landed in France on D-Day, June 6, 1944.

Casualties were heavy as Canadians fought determinedly along the French coast.

In October, Ralston warned King that the fighting had been more intense than anticipated. He sensed that Canadian combat soldiers were bitter about keeping a large and idle standing army in Canada while they were short of reinforcements.

But efforts to induce the N.R.M.A. men to enlist for overseas service failed; Ralston pressed the government for conscription.

King continued to resist conscription.

J.L. Ralston

His cabinet was now ir-reconcilably divided on the question; meanwhile, bitter prejudice was being worked up in the nation against French-Canadians.

Ralston stood by his pro-conscription position, and King suddenly asked for his resignation. General A.G.L. McNaughton replaced him, promising that he could raise the required soldiers through voluntary enlistment.

King and McNaughton tried to persuade N.R.M.A. men to volunteer for overseas service. In less than a month they were forced to admit failure, and a quota system was devised to conscript the personnel necessary.

By the time Canadians were finally conscripted in December, 1944, an Allied victory was inevitable.

Canadian tanks enter San Pancrazio, Italy

In January, 1945, the British and American chiefs of staff offered General Eisenhower valuable reinforcements for his major thrust across northwest Europe. Two Canadian divisions joined the rest of the Canadian army under General Simonds to participate in the final assault.

On May 7, 1945, Germany capitulated, and the war in Europe was over.

King spoke to his people from the San Francisco Conference, where the charter of the United Nations would be drafted.

Jubilantly, King broadcast the news of the Allied victory to his fellow Canadians. Always mindful of making political points, King, who had already called an election for June, claimed his broadcast had been "worth more than two weeks campaigning."

German children surrendering to Canadian troops

King's mystique as a political winner, and the unswerving support of Quebec, combined to give the Government a narrow victory.

It had helped that the Government had passed the Family Allowance Act in 1944. During the election campaign King was able to promise a broader government programme of social security and increased economic planning.

He had also promised public works and gener-ous financial assistance for returning veterans. King had little to say, however, about foreign affairs.

But King was out of step with his cabinet over external affairs.

The world was polarizing into two powerful political blocs: one dominated by the Soviet Union, the other by the United States. Canada was economically and culturally integrated into the American camp. Younger Liberals wanted to join America in actively challenging communism throughout the world.

King feared communism, but he was always cautious in his foreign policy. By promoting an isolationist policy for Canada, he found himself in conflict with both Louis St. Laurent, his secretary of external affairs and undersecretary Lester B. Pearson.

"One has the sensation of sitting at the side of a volcano," he wrote dejectedly in 1948. He had nightmares about war, and dreamed he was trapped in "an area where there was an explosion likely to take place."

While walking on a summer morning, he saw a terrifying face in the clouds, "like the face of a Chinese dragon...a portent of dread."

Shaving one morning, he saw an eagle and a bear shaped from the lather in his shaving mug. The bear (the Russian emblem) seemed to be crushing the wing of the eagle (the American emblem).

"I'm a sick old dog these days," King told his minister of finance.

In January, 1948, he informed the National Liberal Federation that he would retire for reasons of failing health. Who would take his place, and when?

On April 20, 1948, King surpassed British Prime Minister Sir Robert Walpole's record of 7,619 days in office. Now he felt he could retire at any time. Being obsessed with symmetry, especially numerology, he chose the 5th, 6th and 7th of August for the Liberal convention. The 7th was the 29th anniversary of his own election to the leadership in 1919.

In the weeks before the leadership convention he found it very difficult to write his convention speech. He was filled with sadness at the thought of giving up the party leadership.

Urbane and impressive Louis Stephen St. Laurent was King's choice for a successor.

St. Laurent, a Quebec City corporation lawyer who seemed to symbolize postwar prosperity and stability, had been King's strongest French-Canadian cabinet minister after Lapointe's death in 1941. King used all his influence to insure St. Laurent's election.

At the convention his thoughts were of grandfather Mackenzie, Sir William Mulock, his parents and Sir Wilfrid Laurier.

"To me it was very significant...that I should have been piped in to the convention to the tune of Bonnie Dundee. It was there where my grandfather was born and began his early life. It links up the very beginnings of my political life and influences that have served to inspire it with these moments of its close," he wrote at the end of the first day of the convention.

He "kept regretting that I was so completely alone in sharing [sic] the great events of a day like to-day."

It was the closing of an era.

St. Laurent won easily on the first ballot, and for the first time in 29 years the Liberals had a new leader. King's last words to the convention were: "Mesdames, messieurs: Je vous remercie de tout mon coeur."

"It was interesting," he later commented innocently, that "they should have been in French." The old man had seen the fulfillment of his mission. He told the press: "I regarded having helped to keep Canada united throughout the war as the main contribution I had made."

Outside the convention hall a brilliant summer sun began to sink into the evening sky. "I have never seen the Western sky so completely aglow with fire coloured light," King recorded in his diary, "[it] seemed to me a symbol..."

In less than two years, Mackenzie King was dead.

Louis St. Laurent stands over King's coffin

Thousands of Canadians of all walks of life stood in line for hours under the pealing bells of the Peace Tower for the privilege of passing through the arches of the Hall of Fame to where the body lay in state.

Royal Canadian Mounted Police pallbearers carried the body of the former prime minister into Union Station, Ottawa, to be placed on board a special funeral train to Toronto for burial in Mount Pleasant Cemetery.

In his last few years of life, in failing health, Mackenzie King often dreamed about taking a journey. In most of these dreams, or "visions" as he usually called them, he was in a state of anxiety, and in many, a train symbolized the final journey. He worried that the trains would leave before he was ready. Significantly, in one dream, he was waiting for the train alone. Although he could not understand the "vision," he commented bitterly that he was waiting alone because of the work he had done.

In Toronto, thousands
lined the streets to view
the funeral cortege that
made its way slowly
through the streets, hop-
ing to catch a last glimpse
of the man who for over 21
years had been Canada's
prime minister.

How had Canadians seen Mackenzie King?

His technique, his style, did not endear him to most Canadians. Professor Frank R. Scott said of King:

"He blunted us
We had no shape
because he never took sides,
And no sides
Because he never allowed them to take shape.

"He skilfully avoided what was wrong
Without saying what was right,
And never let his on the one hand
Know what his on the other hand was doing.

"Truly he will be remembered
Wherever men honour ingenuity,
Ambiguity, inactivity, and political longevity."

Other Canadians viewed his achievements with reverence.

• He kept French and English Canada together at a critical moment in Canadian history.
• He rebuilt the Liberal party into Canada's strongest and most representative party.
• He helped foster a new sense of Canadian identity.
• He led the country through World War II.
• He initiated progressive social legislation such as family allowances and old age pensions.

He was not a brilliant parliamentarian, but he knew better than any Canadian politician how to juggle conflicting interests and satisfy the majority while appeasing the minority.

He did not and could not unite Canadians with his personal charisma and vision of a national purpose. He dwelt, as all Liberals, on the divisions in the country, and made his way slowly, cautiously, and consciously around them, cajoling and coaxing like a shepherd rather than leading like a general.

Historian Frank Underhill noted of King in the *Canadian Forum*: "His statesmanship has been a more subtly accurate, a more flexibly adjustable Gallup poll of Canadian public opinion than statisticians will ever be able to devise."

Mackenzie King was not loved; he was a pale leader who divided us least.

There was a Mackenzie King few people knew.

To all appearances, King was a lonely old bachelor who took great delight in his morning walks with "Pat" among his Kingsmere ruins. When he retired it seemed he would devote his time to writing his memoirs and using his leisure time to correspond with his friends.

Only after his death, when the 57 years of his diaries were made public, did Canadians begin to understand the other Mackenzie King.

King's spiritualist activities had peaked during the 30's. He tapered off during the war years, but he began to hold séances again during the last three years of his life. These served to reassure him that there was a moral order in the universe, and that he was in harmony with it, fulfilling his mission.

Mrs. Wriedt, King's favourite medium

He was constantly in need of reassurance.

On her deathbed his mother had promised she would never leave him, and to his mind she never had. Every day, all around him, he saw evidence that he was on the right track, and that the spirits of loved ones were with him. His mother's face would appear from the shape of shaving foam in his shaving mug. He would wake up to the sound of hymns from a celestial choir and feel the warm presence of the spirit world.

After the death of his second dog, "Pat," he "repeatedly heard little sounds in my Library as if Pat were there..." Tea leaves would form images in his cup that would reassure him about some decision he had made.

One Sunday after church he chanced to meet a man who told him he had emigrated from Scotland 37 years earlier. Grandfather's rebellion of '37 flooded into his mind. "It was a confirmation again of others making their presence known."

His most frequent source of communication with the spiritual world came from the hands of the clock. Whenever they formed a straight line it indicated to King that he was on the right track. His diary almost daily records his sightings of the clock at appropriate times: ten to four, twenty-two past four, quarter past nine. For Mackenzie King there were no coincidences. "Coincidences...go to prove there are forces at work which we know very little about."

He was close to the spirits.

On the eve of the 1948 leadership convention, Mackenzie King sat alone in Laurier House admiring the paintings of his loved ones and allowing his mind to wander over his remarkable career, now at an end. He thought of father, grandfather and mother. "It was as though that [sic] those that I had loved the most and had meant the most in my life had all gathered around me at that time...In the quiet of that hour, in the peace that was in my mind, my soul roused as it was after speaking, particularly at this moment of great significance in my life. I felt as though we were all together. Cer-

tainly we were in spirit. No one will ever make me believe that they were not all with me at the time...To me, today above all was one of mysticism."

He had come full circle.

Further Reading

The largest source of material relating to Mackenzie King is the King collection at the Public Archives of Canada, which includes his diaries from 1893 to 1950. Copies of most of the diaries are also available at several Canadian university libraries. For his own account of the problems of labour in a capitalist society, King's unreadable *Industry and Humanity* (Toronto, 1919, 1973) may be consulted.

Of the many biographies of King the most concise, fair and popularly written account is J. L. Granatstein's excellent, *Mackenzie King, His Life and World* (Toronto, 1977). The most thorough treatment of King is given in the three volumes begun by Robert MacGregor Dawson, (Toronto, 1958) and continued by H. Blair Neatby, (Toronto, 1958, 1963) and (Toronto, 1976). An invaluable source for the period 1939-48 is the edited diaries, *The Mackenzie King Record, Vols.*

I-IV, by J. W. Pickersgill. H. S. Ferns and B. Ostry have attempted to assassinate King's character in *The Age of Mackenzie King: The Rise of the Leader* (London and Toronto, 1955), but the work is an interesting chronicle of King's association with John D. Rockefeller Jr. and his interests. A fascinating treatment of King's private life is C.P. Stacey's, *A Very Double Life* (Toronto, 1976). Stacey has had the courage and the skill to produce the only in-depth examination of King's very bizarre private world. Bruce Hutchison's overly-sympathetic *The Incredible Canadian* (Toronto, 1953) is a competent popular biography.

Biographies of certain of King's contemporaries can provide insight into King and Canadian politics during his lifetime. Among the best are O. D. Skelton, *Life and Letters of Sir Wilfrid Laurier* (Toronto, 1921), W. R. Graham, *Arthur Meighen* (Toronto, 1960), Neil McKentry, *Mitch*

Hepburn (Toronto, 1967) and Kenneth McNaught, *A Prophet in Politics* (Toronto, 1959).

While biographies are an essential source of political history, the King era cannot fully be understood without reference to certain key social and political studies of the period. For the most general reference, see Kenneth McNaught, *The Pelican History of Canada* (Markham, 1976) or Ramsay Cook, John Saywell and John Ricker, *Canada: a Modern Study* (Toronto, 1964). Donald Creighton's *The Forked Road* (Toronto, 1976), though unsympathetic to King, is a thorough and readable social and political history for the period 1939-1957, which concentrates on Canadian-American relations. For the 20's, W. L. Morton's *The Progressive Party in Canada* (Toronto, 1950) is indispensable. A deeply moving account of the agony and hardship of the 30's is presented with unforgettable impact in Linda

Grayson and J. M. Bliss, eds., *The Wretched of Canada: Letters to R. B. Bennett 1930-35* (Toronto, 1971). Walter Young's *The Anatomy of a Party: The National C.C.F.* provides both a clear history of the C.C.F. and insight into party organization.

Finally, Mackenzie King has left a physical legacy. The Kingsmere estate, including Moorside and the ruins, is open to the general public. Laurier House has become a national museum.

Photo Credits

All photographs courtesy of the Public Archives of Canada, Ottawa, except for the following: *Saturday Night*, 12. Queen's University Archives, 15. Metropolitan Toronto Library Board, 15, 16. University of Toronto Archives, 26, 27, 31, 35. City of Toronto Archives, James Collection, 34, 41, 48, 62, 64, 81, 97, 148, 149, 179. City of Toronto Archives, Public Works Collection, 47. The National Gallery of Canada, Ottawa, 98. The Toronto Stock Exchange, 118. Toronto Star Syndicate, 162, Gilbert A. Milne, Toronto, 170, 173. Toronto Sun Syndicate, 108, 119.

Index